JAMES OGLETHORPE, THE FOUNDER OF GEORGIA

Published @ 2017 Trieste Publishing Pty Ltd

ISBN 9780649113323

James Oglethorpe, the founder of Georgia by Harriet C. Cooper

Except for use in any review, the reproduction or utilisation of this work in whole or in part in any form by any electronic, mechanical or other means, now known or hereafter invented, including xerography, photocopying and recording, or in any information storage or retrieval system, is forbidden without the permission of the publisher, Trieste Publishing Pty Ltd, PO Box 1576 Collingwood, Victoria 3066 Australia.

All rights reserved.

Edited by Trieste Publishing Pty Ltd.
Cover @ 2017

This book is sold subject to the condition that it shall not, by way of trade or otherwise, be lent, re-sold, hired out, or otherwise circulated without the publisher's prior consent in any form or binding or cover other than that in which it is published and without a similar condition including this condition being imposed on the subsequent purchaser.

www.triestepublishing.com

HARRIET C. COOPER

JAMES OGLETHORPE, THE FOUNDER OF GEORGIA

Appletons'
Historic Lives
Series

JAMES OGLETHORPE

APPLETONS' SERIES OF
HISTORIC LIVES.

Father Marquette.
   By REUBEN GOLD THWAITES, Editor of "The Jesuit Relations." Third Edition.

Daniel Boone.
   By REUBEN GOLD THWAITES. Third Edition.

Horace Greeley.
   By WILLIAM A. LINN, for many years Managing Editor of the "New York Evening Post."

Sir William Johnson.
   By AUGUSTUS C. BUELL, Author of "Paul Jones, Founder of the American Navy."

Anthony Wayne.
   By JOHN R. SPEARS, Author of "History of the American Slave Trade," etc.

Champlain: The Founder of New France.
   By EDWIN ASA DIX, M. A., LL. B., Formerly Fellow in History of Princeton University, Author of "Deacon Bradbury," "A Midsummer Drive Through the Pyrenees," etc.

James Oglethorpe: The Founder of Georgia. By MISS HARRIET C. COOPER.

George Rogers Clark.
   By REUBEN GOLD THWAITES. [*In preparation.*]

Each 12mo. Illustrated. $1.00 net.
Postage, 10 cents additional.

D. APPLETON AND COMPANY, NEW YORK.

James Oglethorpe

THE FOUNDER OF GEORGIA

BY

HARRIET C. COOPER

Illustrated

NEW YORK
D. Appleton and Company
1904

To

THE CHILDREN OF GEORGIA

PREFACE

WASHINGTON is no better entitled to be called the Father of his Country than Oglethorpe is to the same distinction with reference to the State which he founded. It is unfortunately true that his life, his achievements, and his character are not as well known to the people of Georgia as they should be, and in the hope of familiarizing the youth of the State with them this book was written.

The influence of a noble life is great and far-reaching, but extends only to those who have been made to know it. The office of biography is to body forth those great personalities to the world, and the larger intent of this work is to extend to the uttermost the inspiring effect of the character of General James Edward Oglethorpe.

CONTENTS

CHAPTER		PAGE
	Preface	vii
I.	Ancestry and Early Years	1
II.	Parliament and Prison Reform	8
III.	Arrival in Savannah	20
IV.	Indians and the Coast Islands	29
V.	Immigration	37
VI.	Return to England	46
VII.	Parliament and the Slave Trade	53
VIII.	Troubles among the Settlers	63
IX.	Indian Troubles	70
X.	Charles Wesley and Other Complications	78
XI.	Affair with the Spaniards	84
XII.	With the Spanish Commissioners	91
XIII.	Commander-in-Chief in Carolina and Georgia	98
XIV.	Journeys to the Interior	109
XV.	Troubles in Florida	118
XVI.	Attack on the Florida Forts	131
XVII.	Peace and the Coming of Whitefield	139
XVIII.	War with the Spaniards again	153
XIX.	After the War	177
XX.	Return to England—The Pretender	186
XXI.	Old Age and Death	197
	Authorities Consulted	210
	Index	213

LIST OF ILLUSTRATIONS

	FACING PAGE
James Oglethorpe	*Frontispiece*
Tomo Chichi	24
Jerusalem Church, Ebenezer, Georgia	44
Savannah in 1734	58
Charles Wesley	80
George Whitefield	144
Fort San Marcos, now called Fort Marion	182
Samuel Johnson	198

JAMES OGLETHORPE

CHAPTER I

ANCESTRY AND EARLY YEARS
1689-1718

The Margravate of Azilia had not been successful. Notwithstanding the declaration of Sir Robert Montgomery that it was "the most amiable country in the universe," and that "paradise with all its virgin beauties is at most but equal with its native excellencies," yet Azilia remained unpeopled, and Sir Robert gave up his Utopian scheme.

That was in the year 1717. The struggling colony of Carolina had attracted the attention of this English nobleman; the hope of adding to his fortune, while ignorant of the difficulties to be overcome, had inspired the scheme of planting a colony which should be at once lucrative to himself and to the colonists. Theoretically, Sir Robert's plans were perfect. He would obtain a grant of lands lying between the rivers Altamaha and Savannah, and bring out at his own expense and within three

James Oglethorpe

years a considerable number of families to settle this future Eden.

He further mapped out the 256,000 acres in symmetrical squares of one mile each, with a continuous projecting line of defenses, so secure that no savage dare molest or make afraid. At the very beginning the colonists should enjoy safety, liberty, and comparative wealth. There remained only one step to secure the foundation of the colony of Azilia—that was, obtaining the colonists. A broad and deep ocean rolled between England and America; contrary winds must be encountered; a long voyage of weeks or months; a parting for life from all they loved in Old England; a home to be made among savages—all this made many shrink back and decline Sir Robert's fair offer. And so it came to pass that Georgia was not called "Azilia," nor does it glory in Sir Robert Montgomery as its founder.

In 1729 Sir Alexander Cuming, one of the victims of the South Sea Bubble—visionary, of course, and apparently anxious for another catastrophe—proposed to build on the Bermuda Islands a college to educate Indians. The scheme fell through for want of Indians—not one in Bermuda, nor ever had been. Sir Alexander must needs look farther west, and turned toward what was called the won-

Ancestry and Early Years

derful Cherokee country, asserting that its fabulous riches could pay England's debt in twenty years.

Sir Alexander was finally sent as an embassy to these Cherokees, and succeeded, after some months, in convincing two head warriors and a conjurer of his importance and the power of England. They acknowledged the King's rule and Sir Alexander as their head. Warriors, Beloved-men, Conjurers assembled, and, placing him on a high seat, formed a circle around him with thirteen eagles' tails, sang all day their war songs, and fasted. Such an auspicious beginning should have brought worthier results, but our record only states that the following year Sir Alexander returned to England, taking with him seven chiefs, who laid the crown of the Cherokees at his Majesty's feet, and presented to him five eagles' tails and four scalps, which did not go far toward paying England's debt. Yet the "Cherokee country" did not lose its reputation; was destined to be colonized, and what Sir Robert Montgomery and Sir Alexander Cuming had attempted, remained for James Oglethorpe to accomplish.

Oglethorpe came of an ancient family, the records showing that before the Normans entered England his ancestors held the estate of

James Oglethorpe

Oglethorpe, in the parish of Bramham. Says Thorsby in his History of Leeds: "Tradition saith that one of the family of Oglethorpe was Reeve (High Sheriff) of the county at the time of the Norman advent, and condemned by the Conqueror for opposing his designs. The ancient seat of Oglethorpe continued in the family till the civil wars when it was lost for their loyalty; and it is said that several of the name died at once in the bed of honor, being slain in a battle near Oxford, of the King's party."

Sutton of Oglethorpe was, on account of his loyalty, "mulcted by Parliament in the sum of £20,000, and his estate eventually fell to the lot of Fairfax." This Sutton was grandfather to our hero. Of his two sons, Theophilus, the younger, entered the army, became lieutenant-colonel, and at the battle of Sedgemoor led the Life-Guards, contributing materially to the victory gained by the royalists. He was honored with knighthood, "attained the rank of major-general and first-equerry to James II, taking command of the army assembled to oppose the Prince of Orange. He was, after the Revolution, deprived of his regiment, but was able to purchase the manor of Westbrook, and married Eleanor, daughter of Richard Wall, Esq., and of Katharine de la Roche, of the Lord Roche family of

Ancestry and Early Years

Ireland, connected by marriage with the Scottish house of Argyle." Sir Theophilus, after serving in two Parliaments, died in his fiftieth year and was buried in Westminster Abbey.

Thus ends the record of the father of Oglethorpe. His mother, Lady Eleanor, who survived her husband thirty years, was in the court of Queen Anne of so much influence, that Swift spoke of her in his coarse way as "a cunning devil." Of her seven children, three were sons. The two elder, Lewis and Theophilus, seem to have made an honorable record in military service and in Parliament, but died young. Thus it was that James Oglethorpe, founder of Georgia, succeeded to the family estate.

Little is known of his early years. From the parish register we learn that he was born June 1, 1689, and was educated in Corpus Christi College, Oxford. Before entering the army he served for a few years as "gentleman volunteer abroad." During that time the incident occurred thus related by Boswell:

When a very young man, only fifteen, serving under Prince Eugene of Savoy, he was sitting at table in company with a prince of the House of Würtemberg, who took up a glass of wine, and by a fillip made some of it fly into Oglethorpe's face. The young soldier was in a dilemma. He durst not

James Oglethorpe

challenge so distinguished a personage, yet he must notice the affront. Therefore, keeping his eye fixed on his Highness, and smiling at the time, as if he took what had been done in jest, Oglethorpe exclaimed: "That's a good joke, but we do it much better in England!" whereupon he flung a whole glass full of wine in the prince's face. An old general present observed, "Il a bien fait, mon prince, vous l'avez commencé"—and thus the affair ended in good humor.

Oglethorpe entered the English army as ensign in 1710, and there remained until peace was made in 1713. In the year following he was made captain-lieutenant of the Queen's Life-Guards, but, preferring active life, soon went to the Continent and enlisted under Prince Eugene. Peace being concluded between the Emperor and the Sultan, Oglethorpe returned to England in 1718, and for some years resided at Westbrook on the family estate—an estate then valued at nearly a million dollars.

The old mansion still remains, though greatly changed. In front, rich meadow-lands slope gradually to the banks of the River Wey, while in the rear the land rises to a steep height, covered with noble trees and commanding a view of the town of Godalming. A tradition still holds faith in that region that the Pretender was once secreted at Westbrook by

Ancestry and Early Years

Lady Oglethorpe, that he used to walk in the twilight and early morning, wrapped in a large cloak, and some rustics, coming suddenly on the strange figure, thought he was a ghost, which notion was encouraged by Lady Oglethorpe, in order to keep people away. To this day the house is said to be haunted.

CHAPTER II

PARLIAMENT AND PRISON REFORM
1722-1732

In 1722 Oglethorpe, then thirty-three years old, was elected to Parliament from Haslemere, and for thirty years represented that borough. From the first his career was consistent and independent. He spoke frequently and always to the point, yet he was no orator, and was known rather for what he did than for what he said. It is probable that he inherited a sympathy for the Stuarts, yet was ever loyal to the reigning house, and an ardent supporter of the Protestant succession. In Parliament his sympathies were chiefly enlisted in bills which came up for the redress of grievances, and especially for the relief of unfortunate debtors.

At this day we can hardly understand how English law punished alike and thrust into the same dungeon thieves, pirates, murderers, with the man whose crime was debt—debt incurred oftentimes as security for some friend.

Parliament and Prison Reform

The jails of London were a disgrace to humanity. Fever, filth, smallpox, were encountered in common, while inhuman keepers plied thumbscrews and sneered at the sufferings of their prisoners.

One Mr. Castell, a skilled architect and author of a costly work, The Villas of the Ancients, became involved in debt, was arrested, and taken to a "sponging-house" attached to Fleet Prison. Not being able to compromise his debts, nor to satisfy the warden's demand for bribes, he was thrust into a ward in which smallpox was raging. Terrified with fear of the disease, he entreated to be sent elsewhere, even into the jail itself, but in vain. He caught the disease, and soon died, with his last breath charging the warden as his murderer. Castell was well known to Oglethorpe, who at once determined to do his utmost toward putting an end to such national crimes. At the earliest opportunity he brought the subject before Parliament. That body appointed a visiting committee of fourteen members of the House of Commons, with Oglethorpe as chairman.

They promptly inspected the various prisons and presented their reports; "the details of some," says a historian, "were too painful and loathsome to be repeated." In the Mar-

James Oglethorpe

shalsea's low rooms, not sixteen feet square, were confined forty, and even fifty, human beings. "The floor not being sufficient for the sleepers, half of them were suspended in hammocks, and so tainted was the atmosphere that they perished for want of fresh air. The sick wards were still worse. Along the walls boards were laid on trestles; under these boards one tier of sick men lay on the floor, on the dresser was another tier, and in the hammocks overhead another tier still. . . . A day never passed without death, and in spring from eight to ten prisoners died every twenty-four hours. Many well-disposed persons left money for the destitute, but it was confiscated by the jailors." The wardens grew rich on bribes. Investigation proved that Bainbridge received in this way an average of £5,000 yearly. He it was who loaded Sir William Rich with irons because of a dispute with him. The committee ordered his release, but on making another visit found him again in chains. Mr. Oglethorpe, as chairman of the committee, reported the matter to Parliament, and the barbarous warden was himself imprisoned.

Pirates and abandoned ruffians were suffered to mix with the unfortunate debtors. Their conduct became so insufferable that some

Parliament and Prison Reform

decent prisoners attempted to escape. They were detected, and the officers made it an excuse for resorting to the thumbscrew, forcing blood from finger-ends. Afterward they were taken to the strong room, a collar fastened on the neck and screwed until blood gushed from nose and ears and the eyes almost started from the head. Savagery could go little farther, but the inhuman Acton added to these barbarities by chaining the living to the dead, and keeping prisoners for days in the same yard with unburied corpses.

Gradually the committee unearthed these horrors. For several years Oglethorpe's time was occupied with the painful task, but he then had the satisfaction of knowing that he had accomplished much, if not all he desired, for the relief of the unfortunate prisoners, and for the punishment of barbarous jailors. A thorough inspection of the prisons and reforms begun, wiped out to some extent the stain on England's governing power.

Meanwhile Oglethorpe had not neglected other duties, and if in Parliament he was often in the minority, it was because he was battling for the right against the interests of party, or pleading the cause of the oppressed.

While chairman of the committee sent to investigate the condition of prisons and their

James Oglethorpe

inmates Oglethorpe had conceived a plan for helping those prisoners confined merely for debt. Many of them were of respectable connection, and he proposed that the claims of their creditors be compromised on condition of their going as colonists to America and planting a settlement adjoining the Carolinas on the tract of land which Sir Robert Montgomery had described as "in the same parallel as Palestine and pointed out by God's own choice."

The scheme grew until it embraced not only the unfortunate of England, but the persecuted Protestants of Europe. To obtain the necessary means, Oglethorpe sought the co-operation of men of wealth and influence, and in due time, twenty others uniting with him, petitioned the throne for a charter, which was granted June 9, 1732, by King George, for whom the colony was to be called Georgia. Oglethorpe then published anonymously some essays calling attention to the proposed emigration, and pointing out the objects and advantage of such a movement. In the third chapter he wrote:

> Let us cast our eyes upon the multitude of unfortunate people in this kingdom, of reputable families and of liberal education; some undone by

Parliament and Prison Reform

guardians, some by lawsuits, some by accidents in commerce, some by stocks and bubbles, some by suretyship; but all agree in this one circumstance that they must either be burdensome to their relations, or betake themselves to little shifts for sustenance which it is ten to one do not answer their purposes, and to which a well-educated person descends with the utmost constraint. These are the persons who may relieve themselves and strengthen Georgia by resorting thither and Great Britain by their departure.

I appeal to the recollection of the reader—though he be opulent, though he be noble—does not his own sphere of acquaintance furnish him with some instances of such persons as have been described? Must they starve? What honest heart can bear to think of it? Must they be fed by the contributions of others? Certainly they must, rather than be suffered to perish. I have heard it said, and it is easy to say so, "Let them learn to work; let them subdue their pride and descend to mean employments; keep ale-houses or coffee-houses, even sell fruit or clean shoes for an honest livelihood." But, alas! these occupations and many like them are already overstocked by people who know better how to follow them than do those of whom we have been talking. As for laboring, I could almost wish that the gentleman or merchant who thinks that another gentleman or merchant in want can thrash or dig to the value of subsistence for his family or even for himself; I say I could

James Oglethorpe

wish the person who so thinks were obliged to make trial of it for one week—or, not to be too severe, for one day only. He would then find himself to be less than the fourth part of a laborer, and that the fourth part of a laborer's wages would not support him. It must be admitted that before he can learn he may starve. Men whose wants are importunate must try such experiments as will give immediate relief. 'Tis too late for them to begin to learn a trade, when their pressing needs call for the exercise of it.

To the suggestion that such persons were unfitted for the drudgery of agriculture, he replied that in Georgia the land was so fertile as to yield an hundredfold, and they would have it for nothing. "Give here in England," he added, "ten acres of good land to one of these helpless persons, and I doubt not his ability to make it support him; but the difference between no rent and rack-rent is the difference between eating and starving. . . . The unfortunate will not be obliged to bind themselves to a long service to pay for their passage, for they may be carried *gratis* into a land of liberty and plenty, where they will find themselves in possession of competent estates, in a happier climate then they knew before; and they are unfortunate indeed if they can not forget their sorrows."

Parliament and Prison Reform

The trustees fully concurred with Oglethorpe in these views, believing, as they said, that "there are many poor unfortunate persons in this country who would willingly labor for their bread if they could find employment and get bread by laboring." They generously had inserted into the charter clauses restraining them from receiving any salary, fee, perquisite—any profit whatever—or from obtaining any grant of lands within the district, either themselves or in trust for them. "No colony," wrote Southey, "was ever established on principles more honorable to its projectors."

They also set the example of contributing largely of their private means, and so charitable, wise, and unselfish were their plans that contributions came from people of every rank, from public institutions, and from Parliament, which granted them the sum of £10,000. A letter was received from far-off Pennsylvania enclosing £100 from William Penn, and very highly approving their undertaking, promising all the assistance in his power.

Dr. Hewatt, a Scotch minister from Charleston, thus expressed the feelings of many: "The benevolent founders of the colony of Georgia may challenge the annals of any nation to produce a design more generous and

James Oglethorpe

praiseworthy. They voluntarily offered their money, their labor, and time for promoting what appeared to them the good of others, having nothing for reward but the inexpressible satisfaction arising from virtuous actions." Tracts were now distributed describing the climate and products of the happy land. The poet Waller pictured it a veritable Eden, declaring in his enthusiasm:

> Heaven sure hath kept this spot of earth uncurst,
> To show how all things were created first.

The funds raised were to feed, clothe, arm, and transport to Georgia such poor people as they should select from those who offered to go. An account was opened with the Bank of England, where a register was kept of the benefactors and their donations. They also bound themselves to make an annual statement of receipts and expenditures before the Lord Chancellor and chief of the courts. Arrangements being completed, the trustees now announced that they were ready to receive applications from those who wished to emigrate. A committee was appointed to visit the jails and obtain the discharge of such poor prisoners as were worthy, carefully investigating *character, circumstances, and antecedents*. Stevens, in his History of

Parliament and Prison Reform

Georgia, referring to the Gentleman's Magazine of London, 1732, and to the manuscript Journal of the Trustees, concludes that "in this selection the trustees exhibited peculiar care and discrimination. They required good moral characters, and examined into the causes and conditions of the misfortunes of each. They confined their charity to such only as fell into misfortunes of trade, and admitted none of those who could get a subsistence in England. They suffered none to go who would leave wives or families without support, none who had the character of lazy or immoral men, and would go without the consent of their creditors." Colonel Charles Jones, considered by Bancroft "the best historian America ever had," says of this painstaking selection of colonists for Georgia:

> Other American colonies were founded and augmented by individuals coming at will, without question, for personal gain, and bringing no certificate of present or past good conduct. Georgia, on the contrary, exhibits the spectacle, at once unique and admirable, of permitting no one to enter her borders who was not deemed, by competent authority, worthy the rights of citizenship.

A common seal was adopted. On one side was the genius of the colony, a figure repre-

James Oglethorpe

senting Liberty. Spear in one hand, cornucopia in the other, she was seated between two rivers, which formed the northern and southern boundaries, and surrounded by the words "Colonia, Georgia, Aug." On the reverse were silkworms at work and the motto "Non Sibi, Sed Aliis," thus representing the disinterested motives of the trustees, and also the special industry they had in view. Having learned that the mulberry was indigenous to Georgia and the climate suitable for the silkworm, they had decided that the silk industry would furnish the most suitable employment for the women and children, the old and infirm, leaving harder and more necessary work for the laborers. Experts from Italy were engaged to teach the best methods of feeding worms and winding silk from cocoons. Oglethorpe had before endeavored to encourage silk-weaving in England, and now proposed to produce in this new colony the raw material.

As they would be exposed to attacks from both Spanish and Indian enemies, they should be soldiers as well as planters. Accordingly they were provided with arms, and, until their departure, daily drilled by sergeants of the Royal Guards. For the same reason it was thought best to establish such a tenure as would equalize the number of soldier-planters, and

Parliament and Prison Reform

place the number of land lots within a narrow compass. Each lot was to be held as a military fief, and to consist of just sufficient land for a comfortable support. Fifty acres was considered enough for a farmer and his family.

It was also determined to prohibit slavery within the province: first, because they would not require such heavy labor as to make the assistance of negroes necessary; second, because if any were permitted at their own expense to import slaves, it would discourage, perhaps ruin, the poor people who were to form the strength of the colony. Thirty-five families, numbering one hundred and twenty persons, were selected. Among them were men of various trades, all of whom were supplied with implements.

CHAPTER III

ARRIVAL IN SAVANNAH
1733

On the 16th of November, 1732, the emigrants embarked at Gravesend on the ship Anne. Oglethorpe, who had so earnestly planned and worked for the good of these unfortunate people, determined to go with them, share their dangers and fatigues, and watch over the establishment of the young colony. He was then in the prime of life, tall, manly, and dignified, said to be "the beau-ideal of an English gentleman, and blessed with ample means for the gratification of every reasonable desire, yet he resolved for a time to deny himself those pleasures for which his nature fitted him, and to become the associate of the poor and ignorant." Doubtless it required more real manliness, more moral courage, than to charge an enemy. Many called him quixotic, romantic, foolish. The foolishness was, however, very deliberate and the romance noble.

Oglethorpe had undertaken the work on the

Arrival in Savannah

condition that he was not to receive any salary or other recompense, but was authorized by the trustees to act as Colonial Governor. They accompanied him to the ship, bade him good speed, and the day following the Anne, with its 120 emigrants and their leader, put out to sea. Oglethorpe had not only furnished his cabin and supplied provisions for himself and servants, but during the voyage largely contributed to the comfort of his fellow passengers. For two months they sailed toward the west, arriving January 13th in the harbor of Charleston, S. C., where "they thanked God and took courage." Their last Sabbath in Old England had been spent together in prayer, so their first in their new home was devoted to earnest prayer and thanksgiving.

The sister colony of South Carolina warmly welcomed them, and with good cause. They were to be a protection against her Spanish enemy to the south. The Governor and his council promised all the assistance in his power, and ordered the King's pilot to conduct the ship into Port Royal, some eighty miles southward, from whence the colonists were to be conveyed in small vessels to the river Savannah. They set sail the day following, while Oglethorpe went on to Beaufort, and ascended

James Oglethorpe

the Savannah River to explore the country and select a site for their town. Yamacraw Bluff attracted his attention, and there on the rich delta lands of the Savannah he fixed their place of abode.

During his absence the emigrants had arrived at Beaufort, to which place he returned on the 24th. The Sabbath which followed they celebrated as a day of special thanksgiving, in which the kind people of Beaufort joined. Before their departure Oglethorpe provided for them and their new-made friends a bountiful feast. Among the items mentioned are "four fat hogs, eight turkeys, many fowls, English beef, a hogshead of beer, and a generous supply of wine." We are informed that no one drank to excess, but that subsequently Oglethorpe made stringent laws against the sale of intoxicating drinks.

The feast being over, they set sail for their new home, Savannah—so called after the river flowing past—and landed there on the last day of the month, rejoicing to escape from long confinement on board the vessel. Four tents were set up, while the men went to work to construct with branches of trees additional bowers for present use. Watch-fires were lighted and the weary people retired to rest. Their faithful leader lay upon the

Arrival in Savannah

ground near the central fire, and at his midnight round found all except his sentinels in peaceful slumber. When morning came he called his little band together, to unite with him in fervent thanks to God for his mercy in bringing them safely to the land of their adoption. He gave them also a few words of counsel, warning them most of all against drunkenness, from which some of them had already suffered. In spite of every precaution and law, rum might be brought among them, and he urged them to resist temptation on their own account and for the sake of their Indian neighbors, to whom "fire-water" was invariably fatal. He reminded them that the seed sown by themselves would, morally as well as literally, bring forth fruit for good or for evil in coming generations. "But," said he, "it is my hope that, through your good example, the settlement of Georgia may prove a blessing and not a curse to the native inhabitants."

In a letter to the trustees dated February 10, 1733, Oglethorpe thus describes the situation of Savannah:

> The river here forms a half-moon, around the south side of which the banks are about forty feet high, and on the top a flat, which they call a bluff. The plain, high ground extends into the country about five or six miles, and along the river for about

James Oglethorpe

a mile. Ships that draw near twelve feet of water can ride within ten yards of the bank. Upon the riverside, in the center of the plain, I have laid out the town, opposite to which is an island of very rich pasturage, which, I think, should be kept for the trustees' cattle. The river is pretty wide, the water fresh, and from the quay of the town you see its whole course to the sea, with the island of Tybee, which forms the mouth of the river. For about six miles up into the country the landscape is very agreeable, the stream being wide and bordered with high woods on both sides.

The colonists were charmed with this new country. Its groves of live-oak, bay, cypress, sweet-gum, myrtle, and tupelo were vine-covered or draped in long gray moss, while the yellow jasmine trailed its odorous clusters over the shrubs which overhung the bluff, and the gayest of birds filled the woods. No lovelier spot had they ever seen, and no suspicion of malarial air or lurking foe troubled them as they set to work. Oglethorpe was wiser, and while everywhere planning and encouraging, thought it important to obtain at once the consent of the natural owners of the soil to the settlement of the colony among them. To this end he sought an interview with Tomo Chichi, the chief of the Yamacraws, who lived two or three miles farther up the river. There Ogle-

TOMO CHICHI, CHIEF OF THE YAMACRAWS, AND
TOOANHOWI, HIS NEPHEW.

Arrival in Savannah

thorpe went, taking with him an interpreter, one Mary Musgrove, an Indian woman who had married a Carolina trader. This woman proved very useful on account of her influence with the Indians, and Oglethorpe afterward gave her £100 yearly for her services. It was not until after Oglethorpe's time that she gave serious trouble to the colony.

The interview with Tomo Chichi was satisfactory, but he stated that there were larger and more warlike tribes just beyond his own, whose consent must be gained to the proposed compact, and he furthermore agreed to invite a deputation of these tribes to hold a conference in Savannah with this people from across the great sea. In Oglethorpe's next letter to the trustees he wrote as follows:

This province is much larger than we thought, being one hundred and twenty miles from this river to the Altamaha. The Savannah has a very long course, and a great trade is carried on by the Indians, there having above twelve trading boats passed since I have been here. There are in Georgia, on this side the mountains, three considerable nations of Indians—one called the Lower Creek, consisting of nine towns, or rather cantons, making about one thousand men able to bear arms. One of these towns is within a short distance of us, and has concluded a peace with us, giving us

James Oglethorpe

the right of all this part of the country; and I have marked out the lands which they have reserved to themselves. Their king comes constantly to church, is desirous to be instructed in the Christian religion, and has given me his nephew—a boy who is his next heir—to educate.

The two other nations are the Uchees and the Upper Creek, the first consisting of two hundred, the latter of eleven hundred men. We agree so well with the Indians that the Creeks and the Uchees have referred to me a difference to determine, which otherwise would have occasioned war.

Our people still lie in tents, there being only two clapboard houses built, and three sawed houses framed. Our crane, our battery cannon, and magazine are finished. This is all we have been able to do by reason of the smallness of our number, of which many have been sick, and others unused to labor, though I thank God they are now pretty well, and we have not lost one since we have arrived here.

The people of Carolina were, for various reasons, much interested in the Georgia colony, and several gentlemen made a canoe voyage from Charleston to this new settlement at Savannah. From the South Carolina Gazette the following extract is taken, which gives their impressions of the leader of the colony:

Mr. Oglethorpe is indefatigable, and takes a vast deal of pains. His fare is but indifferent, having little else at present but salt provisions. He

Arrival in Savannah

is extremely well beloved by the people. The title they give him is *Father*. If any of them are sick, he immediately visits them and takes great care of them. If any difference arises, he is the person who decides it. Two happened while I was here and in my presence, and all the parties went away to all outward appearance satisfied, and contented with the determination. He keeps a strict discipline; I neither saw one of his people drunk, nor heard one swear all the time I have been here. He does not allow them rum, but in lieu gives them English beer. It is surprising to see how cheerfully the men go to work, considering they have not been bred to it. There are no idlers, even the boys and girls do their part. There are four houses already up, but none finished; he hopes that he has got more sawyers to finish two houses a week. He has plowed up some land, part of which is sowed with wheat, which is come up and looks promising. He has two or three gardens which he has sowed with divers sorts of seeds and planted thyme with other pot-herbs, and several sorts of fruit-trees. He was palisading the town around, including part of the common. In short, he has done a vast deal of work for the time, and I think his name deserves to be immortalized. . . . The Indians who are thereabouts are very fond of Mr. Oglethorpe and assist him what they can; and he, on the other side, is very civil to them.

The Governor of South Carolina sent Mr. Bull to assist in laying out the town. One of the streets still bears his name. Mr. Bull

James Oglethorpe

brought with him four sawyers, who, with the help of the colonists, felled a large number of trees for building more houses. Oglethorpe ordered a few of the finest trees spared, and under a group of pines placed his own tent, where he lived for nearly a year, refusing to take possession of even a hut for his own use.

Amid all the work he found time to lay out a public garden, designed as a nursery for supplying the colonists with white-mulberry trees, vines, orange and olive trees, and appointed a gardener to care for them. Meanwhile, he superintended the clearing of land, the building of houses, and constructing of fortifications. To each he assigned his proper work, and even women and children were not idle. Said a writer of that day: "He gave at the same time his orders and his example. There was nothing he did not which he directed others to do." His quick eye detected any shirking, but so much was he revered that a gentle reproof recalled them to duty.

CHAPTER IV

INDIANS AND THE COAST ISLANDS
1733

OGLETHORPE now deemed it best to go to Charleston, and there, before the Governor and General Assembly, he made a formal address. After thanking them for their assistance, he said:

Your charitable and generous proceeding, besides the self-satisfaction which always attends such actions, will be the greatest advantage to this province. You, gentlemen, are the best judges of this, since the most of you have been personal witnesses of the dangerous blows this country has escaped from the French, Spanish, and Indian arms. You know there was a time when every day brough fresh advices of murders, ravages, and burnings; when no profession or calling was exempt from arms; when the inhabitants of the province were obliged to leave their wives, their families, their usual occupations, and undergo all the fatigues of war, for the necessary defense of the country; and all their endeavors scarcely sufficient to defend the western and southern frontier from

James Oglethorpe

the Indians. It would be needless for me to tell you, who are much better judges, how the increasing settlements of the new colony on the southern frontiers will prevent the like danger in future. Nor need I tell you how much every plantation will increase in value, by the safety of the province being increased, since the lands to the southward already sell for above double what they did when the new colonists first arrived. Nor need I mention the great lessening of the burdens of the people, by increasing the income of the tax from the many hundred thousand acres of land either taken or taking up on the prospect of future security.

On Oglethorpe's return to Savannah he was pleased to find awaiting him the representatives of the Lower Creeks, which consisted of eight tribes, all speaking the same dialect. These Indians were tall, well-formed men, had unusual skill in hunting, and were also well advanced in their ideas of the rights and duties of man. They had no religious exercises, yet believed in the existence of a supreme being, whom they called Sotolycate— He who sitteth above and said that all nations were descended from two brothers, one white and the other red. They respected old age, and exhibited some tenderness for the sorrowing in that they refrained from speaking of the dead to one who mourned, or of brothers

Indians and the Coast Islands

to one who had lost a brother. To do so was an offense justifying revenge. Suicide was detested as the meanest cowardice. They seemed, moreover, to realize their ignorance and desired to be instructed.

Oglethorpe received them with the same courtesy he would have extended to men of his own nation, explaining that the English desired neither to annoy or dispossess them, but to live in friendship, to obtain from them some land, and to make a treaty of friendship and commerce. Onechachumpa, a giant-like warrior, replied, stating the extent of their territory and power of the tribe, concluding thus:

We acknowledge the superiority of the white man to the red; we are persuaded that the Great Spirit who dwells above and around all has sent the English here for our good; and therefore they are welcome to all the land we do not need.

He then presented eight buckskins—one for each tribe—the best things, he said, they had to bestow, thanking Oglethorpe for his kindness to Tomo Chichi, who it seems for some untold reason had been banished from his tribe, but on account of his wisdom and bravery had been chosen chief of the Yamacraws, a kindred tribe.

James Oglethorpe

Tomo Chichi entered, attended by his warriors. Bowing low, he said:

When these white men came, I feared they would drive us away, for we were weak, but they promised not to molest us. We wanted corn, and other things, and they gave them; and now of our small means we make them presents in return. Here is a buffalo-skin adorned with the head and feathers of an eagle. The eagle signifies speed, the buffalo strength. The English are swift as an eagle and strong as a buffalo. Like the eagle they flew hither over great waters, and like the buffalo nothing can withstand them. But the feathers of an eagle are soft and signify kindness; and the skin of the buffalo is covering and signifies protection. Let these, then, remind them to be kind and protect us.

The terms of the treaty were soon agreed upon, and consisted, on the part of the English, of fair and just stipulations concerning traffic, reparation for injuries, and so forth; and, on the part of the Indians, a formal ceding to the trustees all the land south of the Savannah as far as the Ogeechee, with lands on the coast from the Savannah to the river Altamaha, extending westward as far as the tide flowed, and all the islands except a few which they reserved for hunting, fishing, and bathing, besides a tract on the margin of the river for

Indians and the Coast Islands

their encampment when visiting friends in the neighborhood.

A very important part of the conference came at the conclusion, when Oglethorpe presented each chief with a laced coat, and hat, and shirt, each war-captain a gun with ammunition, to the "beloved men" mantles of coarse cloth, besides smaller presents to the attendants. The Indians departed highly pleased, promising "to keep the talk in their heads so long as the sun should shine or the waters run into the sea."

Oglethorpe intended making a tour through the northern colonies. Governor Belcher of Massachusetts had some time previous extended an urgent invitation from the Legislature of his Colony, as well as from himself. "It is with great pleasure," he wrote, "that I congratulate you on your safe arrival in America, and I have still greater in the advantages which these parts will reap from your noble and generous pursuits of good to mankind in the settlement of Georgia. May God Almighty attend you with his blessing and crown you with success."

But Oglethorpe did not accept the kind invitation; the young colony needed his attention and he gave up the expected pleasure. He made instead an excursion into the interior,

James Oglethorpe

attended by Captain McPherson with a detachment of rangers. After going forty miles westward, Oglethorpe selected a site on which to build a fort to command the passes through which the Spanish Indians traveled when they invaded the Carolina colony. This fort was soon afterward built, and, in honor of his early patron, named Fort Argyle. His main object was, of course, to protect his own colony from invasion by the Spaniards of Florida. There Captain McPherson was subsequently stationed.

Oglethorpe now returned to Savannah, and upon his arrival called together the inhabitants. According to his custom, before beginning any important work, he joined them in a devotional service, and then proceeded to divide the town into wards and assign the lots. In this work he looked to the future, and although the inhabitants then numbered only *one hundred and twenty,* he laid out the town as for a populous city, with large squares for markets and other public needs, with wide and regular streets crossing each other at right angles and shaded by fine trees. Even in his own lifetime he realized the wisdom of thus acting according to the motto chosen for their seal, "Not for ourselves, but others." The morning's work being con-

Indians and the Coast Islands

cluded, all were invited to a substantial dinner. The afternoon Oglethorpe devoted to opening a court, when, by virtue of his commission, he nominated a recorder and other magistrates; a session was held, a jury selected, and cases tried. Hitherto Oglethorpe had exercised undivided authority over his people, but their increasing numbers made it necessary to delegate to others some of this work.

It was about this time that a colony of Israelites arrived from London, coming at their own expense. Some persons in England were offended at this, refusing any further aid to the colony if the Hebrews were allowed to remain. Oglethorpe was appealed to, and, in reply, praised the good conduct of the Hebrews, especially commending the skill of one Dr. Numis, who since his arrival had rendered valuable aid to the sick among the colonists, making no discrimination between Jew and Gentile. Very wisely, therefore, Oglethorpe refused to remove them; he had no fancy for persecution, and time proved these Israelites to be among the most moral and industrious of Savannah's citizens.

On January 23, 1734, Oglethorpe with sixteen attendants started on another exploring tour, this time among the islands on the southern coast. At St. Simons they stopped to

James Oglethorpe

make an observation of the latitude, and afterward discovered an island which Oglethorpe named Jekyll, in honor of his old friend Sir Joseph Jekyll, master of the rolls and knighted by George I. On the return of this exploring party they ascended the Ogeechee River, and stopped at Fort Argyle, found it well finished and mounted with several guns.

This excursion convinced the Governor that for the sufficient defense of his colony there must be a military station near the mouth of the Altamaha, and a strong fort for an outpost upon the island of St. Simons, and it was upon a high bluff at the western side of this island that Frederica was afterward built. Meanwhile the population of the colony had increased by the arrival of new immigrants.

CHAPTER V

IMMIGRATION
1734

THE Tyrolese valleys of Austria had for many a year sheltered a quiet, God-fearing people, busy with toy-making, wooden clocks, and salt-works. Salzburg was the archbishop's city. Far up among the beautiful mountains it lay, happy and prosperous, until a new bishop arose burning to trample out all sign of Protestantism. Those Bible-reading peasants must choose between the reading and a prison. To prison they went, Bible in hand. And yet the "Right Reverend Father" was not satisfied, since the troublesome Salzburgers asked that they be allowed to get together their small possessions and leave the country, and the Emperor had granted their request.

"Then they must go at once," said the archbishop. And go they did, in dead of night, no clothes, no food. Old men, delicate women, helpless babes, the "Right Reverend"

James Oglethorpe

pushed out into the unknown world, 7,000 the first year, 10,000 the two following. Southey wrote of that sad time:

> But though Catholics shut their gates against them, Protestants lodged them in their houses. The Count of Stolberg dined nine hundred in his palace as they journeyed by; at Leipsic the clergy met them at the gates, and with them entered the town, singing Luther's hymns. The University of Würtemberg went out to welcome them, saying afterward: "We thought it an honor to receive the poor guests." Thirty-three thousand pounds were raised in London for the relief of these Salzburgers, many of whom settled in Georgia—colonists of the best description.

It was in behalf of this persecuted people that Oglethorpe had before addressed Parliament, and he now proposed to the trustees that some of them be offered a home in Georgia. They readily agreed, the invitation was given, by some gladly accepted; and so the Hermanns and Dorotheas were widely scattered. A vessel was sent to convey them to America, where, under the care of Commissary von Reck and their pastors Bolzins and Gronan, they arrived March 7, 1734.

Oglethorpe, who was in Charleston at the time, gave them hearty welcome, and intro-

Immigration

duced them to the Governor of South Carolina, who received them cordially. Nor did Georgia's Governor forget the bodily comfort of his new colonists, but supplied them with fresh provisions and vegetables brought from the gardens of Savannah. A messenger was despatched to that city to announce their coming and direct the magistrates to prepare for their reception.

Two days later the vessel conveying the strangers sailed up the river. They were filled with delight and wonder at the grand forests, the verdure of the banks, the singing birds, and the balmy odor of the pines. The inhabitants of Savannah flocked to the shore and received them with shouts of welcome, to which they heartily responded, and soon landed to enjoy the welcome and the feast prepared for all.

Temporary lodgings were provided until the return of Oglethorpe, who had gone to Charleston intending to embark for England, "but for the love of us Salzburgers," says Von Reck, "he put off this voyage, being resolved to see us settled before he went."

He gave them permission to select a home in any part of the province. With their leaders he went six miles up the river, and from thence fifteen miles through the forest, where

James Oglethorpe

they came to a green valley, well watered by clear brooks, and near the margin of a fine stream eighty feet wide. They were well pleased with the locality and marked the place for a settlement, after which they knelt by the riverside, devoutly thanking God for having brought them safely through great dangers into a land of rest, and in memory thereof naming their new home Ebenezer. Oglethorpe had his own carpenters come to assist in building the houses, while he himself directed them how to lay out the town.

The pastor Bolzins spoke of the Governor as a man having great reverence for God and his Holy Word, adding further:

So blest have been his undertakings and his presence in this land, that more has been accomplished by him in one year than others would have effected in many. For us he hath cared with a most provident solicitude. We unite in prayers for him, that God may guide him home, make his voyage safe and prosperous, and enrich him with many blessings.

Later on the good pastor wrote:

Some time ago I wrote to an honored friend in Europe that the land in this country, if well managed and labored, brings forth by the blessing of God not only one hundred fold, but one thousand

Immigration

fold, and I this day was confirmed therein. A woman having two years ago picked out of Indian corn no more than three grains of rye, and planting them at Ebenezer, one of the grains produced an hundred and seventy stalks and ears, and the three grains yielded to her a bag of corn as large as a coat pocket—the grains whereof were good and full grown, and she desired me to send part of them to a kind benefactor in Europe.

Again, in his quaint way, Bolzins wrote:

As to the present year, we have not been in want of necessary provisions. We have a very hopeful prospect of a good harvest, everything in the fields and gardens growing so delightful as our eyes have hardly seen in this country before.

If Isaac, by the blessing of God, received from what he had sowed an hundredfold, I believe I dare say to the praise of the great mercy of God over us, our Salzburgers will get a thousandfold, notwithstanding that the corn when it came out of the ground was quite eaten up two or three times by the worms.

The land is really fruitful, if the sins of the inhabitants and the curse of God for such sins doth not eat it up, which was formerly the unhappy case of the blessed land of Canaan.

After such glowing accounts, one is surprised to learn that the Salzburgers afterward

James Oglethorpe

became dissatisfied with their location and bent on removing, though they had much ground cleared, a fine range for their cattle, and confessed that they had milk in abundance, fine poultry, with excellent vegetables. Oglethorpe listened patiently to their complaints, and soon discovered that they coveted a spot which the Indians reserved for their own use. That he would not grant, and counseled them to remain where they were, yet gave his permission for them to remove to Red Bluff, on the Savannah River.

This they did, and a quaint old town they made there, said to be much like the Herrnhut of Zinzendorf, thus described by Carlyle: "An opulent enough, most silent, strictly regular little town. The women are in uniform —wives, maids, widows, each their form of dress. Male population, I should think, must be mainly doing trade elsewhere; nothing but prayers, preaching, charitable boarding schooling, and the like appeared to be going on. Herrnhut is a Sabbath petrified; Calvinistic Sabbath done in stone." But we do not find Herrnhut quite like the town these Salzburger brethren established in Georgia, of which the same famous Scotchman says: "There at Ebenezer, I calculate they might go ahead after the questionable fashion of that

Immigration

country, and increase and swell;—but have never heard of them since."

Possibly there are some other things in America of which Carlyle had never heard. Nevertheless, these Salzburgers were heard from in much that was good and praiseworthy. To this day, their county of Effingham owns the influence of those peace-loving Salzburgers, who for many years had no courts of justice, but referred all disputed matters to their pastors and elders, and, if now courts are held there, we are informed that the business, both civil and criminal, is finished in one day!

No vestige of the old town of Ebenezer remains except the church, built of bricks made by the Salzburgers, using lime which they procured from shells found on the Atlantic coast. A stately row of cedars leads from the church to the cemetery, where one finds a monument inscribed to the memory of Bolzins and Gronan, faithful pastors of the church which they had devoutly named "Jerusalem."

> This church [says Strobel, in his History of the Salzburgers] is surmounted by a neat belfry, on top of which is a swan, said to be Luther's coat of arms, and frequently placed on the spires of Lutheran churches in Europe. There is a curious tradition that when John Huss was burned he remarked:

James Oglethorpe

"You this day burn a goose" (Huss signifies goose), "but one hundred years hence a swan will arise whom you will not be able to burn."

There still exists at Bethel a chalice of solid gold, presented to these Salzburgers by the will of a young man who lay dying in Austria. Engraved upon it is this inscription: "Such wishes to the dear Salzburgers in Ebenezer, at every time they partake of the holy communion; by George Matthias Kiderlin, a young man in Nördlingen, who thought of them shortly before his end. . . . Whoever sits down to the table of the Lord with us and our faith, he will be refreshed with the blood of the Lamb of God, and trust in his salvation."

Sad times befell the old church in the days of the Revolution. A recent writer says: "Even now you may see dark rough places on the walls where the plaster refuses to stick, owing to the grease that the bricks absorbed from royal bacon piled up in it during those years. But the crowning indignity came when the soldiers quartered their horses in the sacred place and used it as a stable until the close of the war."

The Salzburgers have gradually amalgamated with the other inhabitants of Georgia, and have furnished many good and noble

JERUSALEM CHURCH, EBENEZER, GEORGIA.
Erected in 1767.

Immigration

citizens to the State. They can be found in nearly every town and county, and are almost invariably among the most highly respected and prosperous. Georgia owes much of her history and her greatness to the colony established at Ebenezer.

CHAPTER VI

RETURN TO ENGLAND
1734

OGLETHORPE'S departure to England had been postponed by the arrival of the Salzburgers. After locating them, he returned to Savannah, placed the colony in charge of Mr. Thomas Causton, storekeeper and bailiff, and, after fifteen months spent in labors for the colony, bade them adieu and started to England. Said one who was present and followed him to the boat: "They could not restrain their tears when they saw him go, who was their benefactor and their father, who had carefully watched over them as a shepherd does over his sheep, and who had so tender care of them both day and night."

He was accompanied by Tomo Chichi, with his wife, his nephew, and his war-captain Hillispilli, besides six chiefs of other tribes, with attendants and an interpreter. Oglethorpe's object in inducing these Indians to go with him was that they might see so much of Great

Return to England

Britain and her institutions as would convince them of her power and dignity.

On March 7th they embarked on the Aldborough, and June 16th arrived at the Isle of Wight, from whence he wrote to Sir John Phillips, Bart., announcing their arrival and telling him of the welfare of the Salzburgers, of whom he spoke as "a very sensible, active, laborious, and pious people," adding as he closed his letter:

> I shall leave the Indians at my estate till I go to the city, where I shall have the happiness to wait upon you and to relate all things to you more fully, over which you will rejoice and wonder.

A grand entertainment was given in honor of the Governor of the Georgia colony, a special meeting was called by the trustees, and a unanimous vote of thanks enthusiastically given for the zeal and ability with which he had managed the settlement. Magazines and papers were full of his praises, a prize poem was called for, even as at this day, and one entitled The Christian Hero won the gold medal, which bore on one side the head of Lady Hastings, and on the other Oglethorpe's, with the words "England may challenge the world." Unfortunately, as we learn from the Gentleman's Magazine of London, 1785, only

James Oglethorpe

a few specimens of this medal were struck off, and the die was destroyed.

The Indians were comfortably entertained at the Georgia Office. Attired in their native costumes with faces painted after the Indian fashion, they were taken to the royal palace, and presented to the King.

Oglethorpe earnestly desired that the Indians be instructed in secular and religious knowledge, and seemed already to have inspired them with like feelings. To increase their desire for instruction, he had induced them to visit England, and now, for their benefit, urged his friend Bishop Wilson to prepare a simple manual of religious instruction, which he could have translated into their language. From a letter previously written, we learn his estimate of Indian character after the fifteen months of intercourse with them. He wrote:

> There seems to be a door opened to our colony toward the conversion of the Indians. I have had many conversations with their chief men, the whole tenor of which shows that there is nothing wanting to their conversion but one to explain to them the mysteries of religion; for as to the moral part of Christianity, they understand it and do assent to it. They abhor adultery and do not approve a plurality of wives. Theft is a thing not known

Return to England

among the Creek nation, though frequent and even honorable among the Uchees. Murder they look upon as an abominable crime, but do not esteem the killing of an enemy, or one who has injured them, as murder.

The passion of revenge, which they call honor, and drunkenness, which they learn from our traders, seem to be the two great obstacles to their becoming Christians. But upon both these points they hear reason.

As for revenge, they say they have no executive power among them, and are forced to kill the man who has injured them in order to prevent others doing the like; but they do not consider any injury, except adultery or murder, deserves revenge. In cases of murder, the next in blood must kill the murderer, or else is looked upon as infamous.

Their kings can only persuade. All the power they have is no more than to call together their old men and captains, and propound to them the measures they think proper. These reason together with great temper and modesty, then call in the young men. They seem to me both in action and expression to be thorough masters of eloquence. In speaking to young men, they generally address the passions; in speaking to their old men, they appeal to reason only. One of the Cherokee nation being come before the Governor, was told he need fear nothing but might speak freely. He answered: "I always speak freely, what should I fear? I am among my friends, and I never feared even my enemies!"

James Oglethorpe

The Gentleman's Magazine of a later day related an incident given by Oglethorpe of an Indian chief, a man after his own heart. When asked by some retreating troops to march with them, he replied: "No! I will not stir a foot till I see every man belonging to me marched off before me; I have always been the first in advancing toward an enemy, and the last in retreating."

Oglethorpe now urged the trustees to send out missionaries. In complying with his desires, they sought eligible men who would go to Georgia to officiate as ministers in Savannah and to instruct the Indians. Among the friends who had most heartily welcomed Oglethorpe on his return to England was the Rev. Samuel Wesley, who addressed him, if extravagantly, yet sincerely, as "Universal Benefactor of Mankind," and in a letter of welcome said:

It is not only your valuable favors to my son Samuel, late of Westminster, and to myself when I was a little pressed in the world, nor to your extreme charity to the poor prisoners, that so much demand my earnest acknowledgments, as your disinterested, unmovable attachment to your country and your raising a new colony—or rather a little world of your own—in the midst of a wild wood where men may live free and happy (if they are not

Return to England

hindered by their own stupidity and folly) in spite of the unkindness of their brother mortals.

John Wesley, a son of this Rev. Samuel, being known to one of the trustees as a man of "abstemious habits and readiness to endure hardships," was by him proposed for this office of missionary. Oglethorpe, although acquainted with the father, was not sufficiently intimate with either of the sons to judge of their fitness for the position. They had gained notoriety at the university by living according to certain strict rules of their own, which gave them the name of "Methodists." John's views were, at that time, unsettled and peculiar. Said his father, writing to his eldest son: "I sat myself down to try if I could unravel John's sophisms, and hardly one of his assertions appeared to me to be universally true."

The board, however, made him the offer. He at first hesitated. His father had recently died, but being encouraged by his mother and advised by his friends to accept, he at length consented. It was afterward decided that his brother Charles should accompany him. Said their pious mother, writing from her home at Epworth: "Had I twenty sons, I would rejoice to see them all thus employed, though I should never see them more."

James Oglethorpe

In the same consecrated spirit she had before written to her son John: "Resolve to make religion the business of your life. I heartily wish that you would now enter upon a strict examination of yourself, that you may know whether you have a reasonable hope of salvation by Jesus Christ. If you have the satisfaction of knowing, it will abundantly reward your pains; if you have not, you will find a more reasonable occasion for tears than can be met with in any tragedy. . . . Would you judge of the lawfulness or unlawfulness of pleasures, take this rule: whatever weakens your reason, impairs the tenderness of your conscience, obscures your sense of God, or takes off the relish of spiritual things—in short, whatever increases the strength or authority of the body over the mind, that thing is sin to you, however innocent it may be in itself."

CHAPTER VII

PARLIAMENT AND THE SLAVE TRADE
1734

PARLIAMENT was at this time in session, and Oglethorpe was not idle. He spoke on various questions, but laws for the benefit of Georgia were nearest to his heart. The first was a bill to prohibit the importation and sale of rum, brandy, and other distilled liquors. In spite of previous efforts, the Carolina traders supplied the Indians and colonists with smuggled spirits, which produced not only disorderly conduct but disease. The bill did not prohibit the use of wine or English beer. A century later Oglethorpe might have learned the danger lurking even in these in that climate, and his broad, unselfish nature would have responded by denying himself lest he "cause his brother to offend."

Another statute which engaged his attention was "an act for rendering the province of Georgia more defensible by prohibiting the importation of black slaves or negroes into the

James Oglethorpe

same." The bill was strenuously opposed. Said the Earl of Dartmouth: "We can not allow the colonies to check or discourage in any degree a traffic so beneficial to the nation."

A tract entitled The African Slave Trade, the Pillar and Support of the British Plantation Trade in America, argued thus: "Negro labor will keep our colonies in due subserviency to the interests of their mother country." The royal instruction from Queen Anne to the Governor had been: "Give due encouragement to merchants, and in particular to the Royal African Company, of England."

It was against this spirit, and against the fact that the other colonies north and south were receiving and owning slaves, that Oglethorpe had to contend. "My friends and I," he wrote afterward, "settled the colony of Georgia, and by charter were established trustees. We determined not to suffer slavery there, but the slave merchants and their adherents not only occasioned us much trouble, but at last got the Government to sanction them." At this period, however, the bill to prohibit the importation of slaves was passed, and not until Oglethorpe had severed his connection with the colony were they brought in.

In the discussion before Parliament the Georgia Governor seemed to stand alone on

Parliament and the Slave Trade

this important question, most of them agreeing with Burke, who remarked: "These regulations, though well intended and meant to bring about excellent purposes, were made without duly considering the nature of the country or the disposition of the people which they regarded."

The Governor of Massachusetts, then a slave-owning colony, was wiser than some of his constituents. Said he: "I insist upon it that the prohibitory regulations of the trustees are essential to the healthy and prosperous condition of the colony."

Two reasons had been given by the trustees for forbidding the purchase of slaves: the vicinity of the Spaniards, who constantly instigated them to insurrections, and the injustice to the white laborer, with whom they would come in conflict. Oglethorpe expressed a higher motive. "Slavery," said he, "is against the Gospel, as well as the fundamental law of England. We refused as trustees to make a law permitting such a horrid crime." A few years later, when some of the colonists requested that slaves be allowed to come in, he sternly refused, declaring that if negroes were introduced into Georgia, "he would have no further concern with the colony."

While Oglethorpe remained in England a

James Oglethorpe

few discouraging reports were sent from Georgia, but on the whole much that was cheering, especially that the people had gathered a fine crop of Indian corn, upward of one thousand bushels, and that Savannah was in a prosperous condition. The trustees received from the Indians a curious missive expressive of thanks for the attention bestowed on Tomo Chichi and his companions. This was the dressed skin of a young buffalo, covered with figures printed in black and red. When delivered in Savannah, it was translated in the presence of fifty chiefs, after which the hieroglyphic skin was sent to England, there framed and hung in the Georgia Office, Westminster.

At this time the silk industry promised well, and from time to time specimens of the raw silk were sent to the trustees. In May, 1735, some of these were exhibited to Queen Caroline, who was so well pleased that she ordered them woven and a dress made, in which she appeared in court on her birthday. It is a matter of surprise and regret that this industry should have been abandoned in the State, when, one hundred and sixty years ago, a Queen of England appeared in Georgia silk!

In this Georgia beehive, as in all busy places, the usual number of drones were found. Neither gratitude to their benefactors nor their

Parliament and the Slave Trade

own future good were sufficient incentives to industry and economy. They really impeded the progress of the more industrious and worthy colonists. The trustees determined for the future to be still more careful to secure only the best class of settlers. More stringent laws were made. From an official report we learn that all applicants were informed that they must undergo great hardships at the first and exercise much industry afterward; that, although they should have lands forever, and free provisions for twelve months, these lands must be cleared and cultivated before they could reap a harvest, and in the meantime they must live chiefly on salt meat, and drink but little water; that they must keep constant guard against their enemies; that the climate was hot in summer and dangerous to those who indulged in spirituous liquors—in short, that the most rigid temperance was necessary to preserve health and substance. With sobriety, industry, and trust in God they could establish homes for themselves and their children; otherwise, they were warned not to emigrate to Georgia.

Some were disheartened and gave up, but their places were filled by a better class. Especially in Scotland had the proposal of the trustees been well received, and 130 Highlanders, with fifty women and chil-

James Oglethorpe

dren, embarked for Georgia, arriving in January, 1736. Lingering a few days in Savannah, they then traveled southward. On the left bank of the Altamaha, about sixteen miles above St. Simons, they selected a town site, calling it after their Scotch home, New Inverness—a name afterward changed to Darien.

The town council of Inverness, Scotland, gratefully expressed their appreciation of the kindness of Oglethorpe to the Highlanders by conferring upon him the honor of a burgess of the town. A greater honor and satisfaction he realized afterward in the services of these gallant and efficient men, among whom were the McKays, the McIntoshes, the McLeods, and their brave countrymen.

Oglethorpe was still in England, making preparations for an even larger embarkation. Two vessels were chartered by the trustees and a sloop of war placed at his disposal. Besides 220 English emigrants, there were sixty more Salzburgers, and some independent adventurers, among whom were Sir Thomas Bathurst and his family.

Besides these Salzburgers, there were, it is recorded, "other poor Protestants of Germany." These, we may suppose, were the Moravians, of whom the Gentleman's Maga-

VIEW OF SAVANNAH AS IT STOOD IN 1734.

Parliament and the Slave Trade

zine said: "In consequence of the oppression which they suffered in Bohemia, the United Brethren, or Moravians, resolved to emigrate to the new colony of Georgia, whither the Salzburgers have already gone." They appealed to Count Zinzendorf, who applied to the trustees and secured for them a free passage and grant of land. "They established themselves," says Hildreth, "on the Ogeechee River, south of Savannah." Of their progress we may quote the following from Grantz's History of the United Brethren: "The Brethren began their settlement in the town near Savannah, and God so blessed their industry that they were not only soon in the capacity of maintaining themselves, but were also serviceable to their neighbors. They erected a schoolhouse for the children of the Indians, on the river Savannah, four English miles above the town. There, King Tschatschi came to see, as he expressed it, 'how they might hear the great Word.' "

This school they rightly named Irene, for their motto was "peace," and with the savages, as with all the world, they were always in peace. Ever industrious, they were especially successful in raising silkworms, producing soon 10,000 pounds a year of raw silk, and also making indigo a staple.

James Oglethorpe

Oglethorpe was sorely tried because of their peculiar belief, which forbade their bearing arms even in the sorest need of the colony, yet he never regretted offering them a home among his people, who could but profit by their upright example. In later years some of them removed to Pennsylvania, settling the towns of Bethlehem and Nazareth, which do honor to their memory. They had prospered in Georgia, and on leaving honorably refunded the money paid for their passage across the sea.

Now we return to those who sailed with these Moravians on October 20th. On account of bad weather the vessels were forced to anchor for some time in the Downs, and again at St. Helens. The delay, with so many persons in idleness, was expensive to the trustees, and the emigrants were losing the most useful season for cultivating their lands. Finally, on December 10th, they put to sea. Oglethorpe chose to go in one of the ships crowded with passengers, that he might be able to care for them on the voyage.

He was well assisted by Mr. Francis Moore, whom the trustees had appointed keeper of the stores. The Wesleys also were with him, and frequently in his cabin. Mr. Wesley said that on one of these occasions the officers and certain gentlemen who had been invited in with

Parliament and the Slave Trade

them took some liberties with the clergymen, not liking their gravity. Oglethorpe was roused at their conduct and exclaimed: "What do you mean, sirs? Do you take these gentlemen for tithe-pig parsons? They are gentlemen of learning and respectability; they are my friends, and whoever affronts them insults me!" The missionaries were treated thereafter with the greatest respect. The voyagers had prayers twice a day, the missionaries catechized the children, and on Sundays administered the sacrament, while the dissenters sang psalms and worshiped in their own way.

Oglethorpe had laid in a large supply of live stock and various dainties, which he shared not only with his friends, but his table was always full, the captain, the missionaries, and others being ever welcome. On February 4th the joyful cry of land was heard, and two days after they anchored near Tybee Island, at the mouth of the Savannah River. Landing on a small island opposite Tybee, Oglethorpe led them to a rising ground, where they all knelt to give thanks for their safe arrival. After showing them how to dig a well and making some other arrangements for their comfort, Oglethorpe left them with their ships and took boat for Savannah, where he was received with a salute of twenty-one guns from the fort.

James Oglethorpe

He was surprised and gratified at the improvements made in the town. Three years before it was a dense forest; now there were two hundred dwellings, some of them two and three stories high. The town was governed by three bailiffs. Laws were made and cases tried as in England, with this difference: "no lawyers were allowed to plead for hire, nor attorneys to make money; but every man pleaded his own cause." The public gardens were the pride of the town, and the Governor was especially pleased with their flourishing condition. The coldest quarter was planted with apples, pears, plums, while in the southern exposure were growing olives, figs, pomegranates, and vines. In one sunny spot was a collection of tropical plants, coffee, cotton, and palma-Christi, which had been sent from the West Indies. A large part of the ground had been planted with white-mulberry trees, forming a nursery from which the settlers were to be supplied in their culture of silkworms.

CHAPTER VIII

TROUBLES AMONG THE SETTLERS
1735-1736

IN the silk industry Oglethorpe was disappointed. The Italians brought from Piedmont went on well for a time, then, quarreling among themselves, one of them destroyed the machines for winding, spoiled many of the eggs, stole more, and ran away to Carolina. No more silk could be wound that year. Oglethorpe ordered the Italian women to teach English girls their part of the work and the men to instruct the gardeners in the care of the mulberry-trees, hoping to start anew the next year.

The view of the river was encouraging. Besides the smaller boats, there lay at the wharf two vessels, one a ship crowded with emigrants; on a large island opposite numbers of cattle grazed; westward, as the river wound through the forest, it flowed past the young towns of Westbrook, Purrysburgh, and other villages; to the south might be seen Highgate

James Oglethorpe

and Hampstead, and eastward the river broadened to the sea, where lay the English shipping.

With great satisfaction the good Governor beheld these improvements, but amid it all did not forget the people lately arrived at Tybee. Already he had ordered refreshments sent down to them, and on the 8th himself returned in a boat laden with fresh beef, pork, venison, wild turkeys, fresh bread, beer, and vegetables.

During his absence some Carolina sutlers had visited the ships and smuggled rum on board, but the officers discovered it and promptly ordered the kegs to be staved. In revenge, the traders spread reports among the immigrants that all who went south would be massacred by the Spaniards and Indians. The Germans, becoming alarmed, begged to be sent to Ebenezer. Captain Hermsdorf, however, expressed his desire to serve with the English to the last.

The Scotch Highlanders were undaunted. "If the Spaniards use us ill," said they, "we will drive them out of their fort, and so have houses ready built to our hands." The Governor assured them that the reports were false, that the Spaniards were at peace with them, and the Indians in alliance. "Still," said he, "caution is the mother of safety, and, there-

Troubles Among the Settlers

fore, it is fitting to keep the men to arms and discipline, and for that reason I shall be glad of your assistance."

After three hours' stay he left them, for there were other settlers whose interests must not be neglected. To assist the Highlanders at Darien he sent fifty rangers and one hundred workmen with Captain McPherson. He appointed surveyors to inspect the country between the Savannah and the Altamaha, with a view to opening a road to Darien; procured for them Indian guides, packhorses to carry provisions, and detailed an officer with a party of rangers to escort them.

On the 12th he again visited the ships at Tybee, and there also came Tomo Chichi with his wife, "Scenaukay," and his nephew, bringing presents of venison, honey, and milk. Being introduced to the missionaries, the old chief said: "I am glad you are come. When I was in England I desired that some one would speak the great Word to me. I will go up and speak to the wise men of our nation, and I hope they will hear. But we would not be made Christians as these Spaniards make Christians, we would be taught before we are baptized." Scenaukay then presented the missionaries with two large jars, one of honey and one of milk, and invited them to Yama-

James Oglethorpe

craw to teach their children, saying the milk represented food for their children, the honey their good wishes. Tomo Chichi informed Oglethorpe that he had kept for two months "runners" awaiting his coming, and on his arrival had sent them to notify the Creeks, and that he had despatched a party of Indians to help the Highlanders at Darien.

He then presented a complaint from the Uchees that, contrary to agreement, cattle had been brought into their territory, and that planters from Carolina had brought negroes and settled therein. Oglethorpe promptly sent orders for them to withdraw within three days both negroes and cattle, or be arrested for trial in Savannah. At the same time he issued a proclamation calling attention to the act for maintaining peace with the Indians.

He had been much troubled by the delay in transporting the new settlers to their future home. The mates of the English vessels were timid, afraid to risk the navigation of Jekyll Sound. To prove that they exaggerated the dangers, he bought at a high price the sloop Midnight with her cargo, on condition that it should be delivered at a station on the Altamaha. He sent on board thirty of the old colonists, trained soldiers, with arms and ammunition, and ordered them to proceed to St.

Troubles Among the Settlers

Simons. He himself, with a few Indians, set out for the same place in a scout boat, and, being in haste, the crew rowed night and day. Though they had stormy weather, the men worked willingly, vying with each other to please their Governor. Said one of the passengers: "He lightened their fatigue by giving them refreshments, which he spared from himself rather than let them want."

The Indians, seeing how hard the crew labored, desired to take the oars, and rowed well, only differing from the others by making a short and long stroke alternately, which they called the "Yamasee stroke." In and out through the passages between the islands skirting the coast, the straits varying in width from two hundred yards to more than a mile, they rowed steadily, reaching St. Simons after two days' travel. There they found the Midnight, and Oglethorpe handsomely rewarded the captain for being the first to enter the port.

Immediately after landing he set all hands to work, making a booth to hold the stores. Digging the ground three feet deep, they threw up earth to form a bank, on which poles were raised to support a roof. The whole was well covered with palmetto-leaves. Similar booths were made for the temporary abode of the

James Oglethorpe

families, and, after a hard day's work, all enjoyed a plentiful feast of game and venison brought in by the Indians. On the three days following Oglethorpe instructed the men in building a fort, digging ditches and turfing the ramparts, and then left them for Darien.

The Highlanders there received him "in martial style, with broadswords, targets, and firearms." "The commanding officer, Captain Mackay, invited him to sleep in his tent and enjoy the soft bed with Holland sheets and plaid curtains, a rare comfort in that part of the world; but he chose to lie at the guard fire, wrapped in his own plaid, for, in compliment to the Scots, he wore a Highland costume."

Possibly Oglethorpe recalled these voluntary hardships when, forty years later, as Boswell relates, he discussed with Dr. Johnson the subject of luxury. "Depend upon it, sir," said Dr. Johnson, "every state of society is as luxurious as it can be; men always take the best they can get." "But," said Oglethorpe, "the best depends much upon ourselves, and if we can be well satisfied with plain things, we are in the wrong to accustom ourselves or our palates to what is high-seasoned and expensive. What says Addison in his Cato, speaking of the Numidian?

Troubles Among the Settlers

Coarse are his meals, the fortune of the chase;
Amid the running stream he slakes his thirst,
Toils all the day, and at the approach of night
On the first friendly bank he throws him down,
Or rests his head upon a rock till morn;
And if the following day he chance to find
A new repast, or an untasted spring,
Blesses his stars and thinks it luxury.

Let us have *that* kind of luxury, sir, if you will."

The Highlanders at Darien had already built a fort and planted four cannon; also a guardhouse, a store, and a chapel.

Several Indians who lived near brought them venison and other game. They were more than friendly, and Spalding, in his memoir of McIntosh, tells us: "The costume of the Highland clansman, his cap and plume, his kilt and plaid, soon became very dear to the red man of the woods. They mingled in their sports and hunted buffalo together— for the woods of Georgia were then as full of buffaloes as the plains of Missouri are now, and the writer of this tale was told when a boy by General Lachlin McIntosh that when a youth he had seen *ten thousand* buffalo within ten miles." After a short visit at Darien, Oglethorpe returned to Frederica, on St. Simons Island, and from there to his immigrants at Tybee.

CHAPTER IX

INDIAN TROUBLES
1736

The island of St. Simons was about fifteen miles long and from two to five broad. A few acres had been cleared by the Indians, the rest was covered with beautiful forests. Wild vines gave promise of future vineyards; game abounded, there being no lack of rabbits, squirrels, partridges, besides the more-desired wild turkey and roebuck.

These were the pleasant things, but it should be added that there were rattlesnakes in the woods, and in the sound frightful alligators. "These so frightened the settlers," says Mr. Francis Moore, "that Oglethorpe once had one brought up into the town of Savannah and encouraged the boys to beat it with sticks that they might not be afraid of the monster."

The season was far advanced, yet Oglethorpe hired laborers who knew the nature of the country to instruct the colonists in plant-

Indian Troubles

ing, with a view to the next season's work. The soil was sandy, with a mixture of rich mold. Good water could be found within ten feet of the surface of the ground.

The Creek Indians had now confirmed their grants of territory, and Tomo Chichi came down with them to point out the boundary-lines. Oglethorpe was not ready to go, therefore the Indians proposed to hunt buffalo on the mainland while waiting. But the Governor feared to trust them, knowing their hatred to the Spaniards, and he suspected that they meant to annoy them. He therefore decided to postpone other matters and go at once, especially as he was growing anxious for the safety of Mr. Dempsey, who had been sent as commissioner to confer with the Spanish Governor of Florida, and had not been heard from.

In two scout boats, with forty Indian warriors and chosen hunters, Oglethorpe set out, leaving Frederica in charge of Captain Hermsdorf. They rowed across Jekyll Sound, sleeping the first night in a grove of pines on the mainland, and the next day reached an island called by the Indians Wisso or Sassafras. Tomo Chichi now changed its name to Cumberland, in honor of the young prince who had been so gracious to them in England. The prince had given to Tooanahowi a gold re-

James Oglethorpe

peater. Holding the watch in his hand, the Indian said: "The duke gave us this watch that we might know how time passes. We will remember him at all times, and therefore give this island his name." Oglethorpe here marked out a fort, to be called St. Andrews, and left Captain Mackay with a few Highlanders to superintend the building.

Rowing on through shoals and narrow passes among the marshes, they came to an island which, for its exceeding beauty, the Spaniards had named Santa Maria. Orange-trees were covered with blossoms, and wild vines clung in profusion to the odorous branches. In honor of the princess of England, Oglethorpe changed its name to Amelia. The next island was the San Juan of the Spaniards, which name they changed to Georgia, after their King. On this was the old fort supposed to have been built by Sir Francis Drake, and Captain Hermsdorf was sent to repair and occupy it.

Climbing some rocky heights, Tomo Chichi pointed out to the governor the St. Johns River, the boundary-line of the Spanish possessions. A house on the farther side, Tomo Chichi said, was the Spanish guard-house. "All on this side the river we hunt," said the chief; "it is our ground. All on the other

Indian Troubles

side they hunt, but they have lately hurt some of our people, and we shall drive them away. We will stay until night behind these rocks, where they can not see us, then we will fall upon them."

It was with much difficulty that Oglethorpe persuaded them not to attack the Spaniards, but to return to the palmetto grounds near Amelia Island, where he promised to meet them. Leaving with them Mr. Horton and one of the scout boats, he went in the other to the Spanish guard-house to inquire what had become of Mr. Dempsey, who had been sent to St. Augustine to treat with the Spaniards. He could see no one in either the upper or lower lookout, and at night returned to the palmetto grounds, where he found all except Tomo Chichi, who had gone on.

In the night the sentinel challenged a boat. An Indian answered, jumped out, and was followed by three others. They were in a terrible rage, and said, in reply to Oglethorpe's questions: "Tomo Chichi has seen enemies, and has sent us to tell you and to help you." "Why did not Tomo Chichi come back?" "Tomo Chichi is an old warrior, and will not come away from his enemies till he has seen them so near as to count them. He saw their fires, and before daylight will be revenged for

James Oglethorpe

the men whom they killed while he was away; but we shall have no honor, for we shall not be there." And their eyes glared with rage over this indignity. When asked if there were many, they said: "Yes, a great many, for they had a large fire on high ground, and Indians never make large fires except when so strong as to defy all resistance."

Oglethorpe ordered all his men into the boats, and rowed rapidly to where Tomo Chichi lay, about four miles away. The old man said he had seen eight white men around a fire, but he believed the Indians had concealed themselves in the woods, and he was bent on attacking them at once. With great difficulty Oglethorpe obtained a short delay, but soon the Indians, thinking it looked like cowardice, determined to go in spite of his commands. "Then," said Oglethorpe, "you go to kill your enemies in the night because you are afraid of them by the day. Now I do not fear them at any time. Therefore wait until day, and I will go with you and see who they are."

This speech had the desired effect. Tomo Chichi sighed, but sat down, saying: "We do not fear them by day, but if we do not kill them to-night they will kill you to-morrow." At daylight they started toward the enemy. A white flag was soon discovered flying on the

Indian Troubles

shore, and, to Oglethorpe's great delight, the supposed enemy proved to be Major Richards, with Mr. Dempsey and his crew, returned from Florida.

Major Richards reported that they had been cast away, had lost their baggage, but men and boat were saved; that they had walked many miles along the sands before reaching St. Augustine, but were finally taken to the Governor, who received them with courtesy. They were compelled to remain a long time to have their boat repaired, but had at last brought with them letters to Oglethorpe from Don Francisco del Morale Sanchey, Captain-General of Florida and Governor of St. Augustine, who desired an answer in three weeks.

The same day all returned to Cumberland Island, where Oglethorpe was well pleased with the rapid progress made by Captain Mackay in the constructions of the fort, especially as the loose, sandy soil made it difficult to raise the work. "They used," said Moore, "the same method to support it as Cæsar mentions in the wars of the Gauls—laying trees alternately with earth, the trees preventing the sand from falling and the sand saving the wood from fire. The Scots who had been aiding in the work were now offered the chance

James Oglethorpe

to return to their settlement, but chose to remain and go on with the task so long as there was any danger.

Oglethorpe, with the Indians, now returned to Frederica, where he called the people together to give them the contents of the Spanish Governor's despatches. These were full of wily compliments, but there were also complaints that the Creeks had attacked the Spaniards, and the Governor desired that "Don Diego Oglethorpe" restrain his Indian allies.

Oglethorpe knew further, by private advices, that, notwithstanding his friendly speeches, the Governor of St. Augustine had sent to purchase arms at Charleston, intending to send his Florida Indians with men from the Spanish garrison to drive the English out of Georgia, and that the complaint against the Creeks was a mere pretext to begin the war.

Oglethorpe determined that there should be no excuse for beginning hostilities, and therefore sent a marine boat and a large periagua of twenty oars fitted out with swivel-guns to patrol the St. Johns and prevent any Creeks from passing to attack the Spaniards. Scout boats were ordered to cruise among the islands to prevent any hostile vessels from entering Jekyll Sound. Tomo Chichi was requested to send messages to the Creeks, de-

Indian Troubles

siring them not to molest the Spaniards until a conference could be held, but to keep upon the mainland and watch lest any Spanish horse pass to Darien. Before the Indians left they had a war-dance. Oglethorpe and his people attended, and presents were given to the red men, with thanks for their faithful service.

CHAPTER X

CHARLES WESLEY AND OTHER COMPLICATIONS
1736

To add to his trials, Oglethorpe found upon his return to Frederica that settlement in a state of turmoil. Charles Wesley, who had come out as a missionary, was also acting as his secretary, and during his absence had, in his zeal to reform various improprieties of the people of Frederica, overstepped the bounds of a minister's privilege. His untimely rebukes, though probably deserved, were quickly resented, for, as Southey remarks, "Charles Wesley attempted the doubly difficult task of reforming some of the lady colonists, and reconciling their petty jealousies and hatreds of each other; in which he succeeded no further than to make them cordially agree in hating him, and caballing to get rid of him in any way."

Oglethorpe had forbidden any shooting on the Sabbath, but the first day of his absence a gun was fired during the sermon. The con-

Wesley and Other Complications

stable ran out and found it was the doctor, who resisted arrest. Whereupon Captain Hermsdorf came with two soldiers and took the important individual to the guard-house. The doctor's wife, who had her own little grudge against Wesley, accused him of causing the arrest, and threatened revenge. Wesley demanded an audience with Lawley, his accuser. He was sent for, and, upon Oglethorpe's close questioning, dropped all his charges except that Wesley had forced the people to prayers.

Other troubles, however, came out of the arrest, again kindling the wrath of the Governor. The people were in such a state of confusion that he said it was easier to govern a thousand than sixty, for in the smaller number every one's passion was considerable, and he durst not leave before all was settled. He still thought that Charles Wesley had, by his indiscretion, excited the disorder, and no explanation effaced the unfavorable impression from his mind.

He well knew the piety of the parents of the missionary, the ability, learning, and self-denial of the young Wesleys, and it was a bitter disappointment that his hopes for their efficient aid in the colony were not realized. His cares were increasing. Amid the building of houses, constructing batteries, getting

James Oglethorpe

supplies, the threatened invasion of the Spaniards made it more necessary that a united people should work together for the good of the colony. A happy reconciliation came soon, after both parties had time for calm reflection free from outside influences.

In the meantime the Governor was actively engaged in strengthening the defenses and providing various things necessary for the comfort of his people. The works around the fort were palisaded with cedar posts, platforms for cannon were laid upon the bastions, a marshy ground below the fort was formed into a "spur" on which guns were placed level with the water and commanding the entrance to the sound.

Having noticed that his guard were growing careless, he one day rowed quietly upstream, landed with his crew, and approached close enough to surprise the sentry, who fled, shouting that the enemy had landed. His men fired a volley and raised the Spanish war-cry, which spread consternation and made every soul fly into the fort, where they remained until, with much chagrin, they learned the truth—that their Governor was testing their vigilance.

On April 13th Major Richards and Mr. Horton were sent with his reply to the Governor

CHARLES WESLEY.

Wesley and Other Complications

of St. Augustine, in which he was informed that armed boats had been sent to patrol the St. Johns, and thus hinder any lawless persons from creating disturbance between the Spaniards and the English.

Oglethorpe had great cause for anxiety, knowing how helpless he was should the Spanish boldly attack him. Not one regular soldier had he in his command to oppose an enemy who had at St. Augustine a garrison of three hundred foot and fifty horse, besides militia and reenforcements daily expected from Havana. This he knew by private advices, and was also informed that a large force had recently marched out of St. Augustine. At the same time came a letter from the Spanish Governor complaining that the Indians had attacked his fort at Picolata and were secretly upheld by the English. Messengers were at once despatched to hasten the coming of a company promised by the Assembly of Carolina, and to the sloop-of-war Hawk, lately arrived at Savannah. At length a small part of the company arrived and were hurried on by Oglethorpe to the eastern end of the island, where he had determined to erect a fort which would command the entrance to Jekyll Sound.

On the 16th news came from St. Andrews that strange ships were seen out at sea, and

James Oglethorpe

several guns heard. Oglethorpe at once called in some parties of Indians, and, ordering them to keep near the town, set every white man to work on the defenses. He built a forge within the fort, a magazine beneath one of the bastions, and laid in a stock of provisions. He then started in an armed boat for St. Andrews, determined to learn for himself the exact state of affairs.

From Wesley's journal we learn that he went with sore misgivings and a heavy heart.

"You will see me no more," said he. "Take this ring and carry it for me to Mr. V——. If there is a friend to be depended on, he is one. His interest is next to Sir Robert's. Whatever you ask within his power, he will do for you, your brother, and your family. I have expected death for some days. These letters show that the Spaniards have been seducing our allies, and intend to cut us off at one blow. I fall by my friends—Gascoigne whom I have made, the Carolina people upon whom I depended to send their promised succors. But death is to me nothing; T—— will pursue all my designs, and to him I recommend them and you."

He then gave Wesley his diamond ring. A reconciliation had been made between the two, and their parting was full of kindly feeling.

Wesley and Other Complications

I attended him to the scout boat, says Wesley, where he waited some minutes for his sword. They brought him first, and a second time, a mourning sword. At last they gave him his own, which had been his father's. "With this sword I was never yet unsuccessful," he said. "I hope, sir," said I, "you carry with you a better, even the sword of the Lord and of Gideon." "I hope so too," he added. When the boat put off, I ran before into the woods to see the last of him. His last word to his people was: "God bless you all!"

CHAPTER XI

AFFAIR WITH THE SPANIARDS
1736

On their way to St. Andrews Oglethorpe and his crew encountered a storm which forced them to seek shelter among the oyster-banks of Jekyll Island. On reaching the island he ordered a ravelin to be added to the fort, a palisade to be made around the base of the hill, and sent a scout boat with assistance to Captain Hermsdorf at Fort St. George.

Sails having been seen out at sea, he took boat again for St. Simons, arriving safely at Frederica. There he found several boats, manned by a number of volunteers, had come from Savannah, having heard that the Spaniards had taken Frederica, and that Oglethorpe was killed.

On Cumberland and Jekyll Islands lookouts had been set to give notice of the approach of shipping. One was reported, but proved to be the sloop-of-war Hawk from Savannah, which soon anchored below the town. Later

Affair With the Spaniards

the scout boat Carolina returned from Fort George. A report was received that Major Richards, who had been sent to the Spanish Governor, had been imprisoned in St. Augustine. Also that Captain Hermsdorf's men had mutinied and compelled him to abandon Fort George.

On May 2d, leaving the fort in command of Captain McIntosh, he started in the scout boat Georgia, accompanied by Lieutenant Moore in a yawl. He was relieved to find no mutiny at Fort St. George, but a panic had been caused by the lies of one man, whom Oglethorpe promptly sentenced to "run the gantlope." The other men were put to work strengthening the old fort, after which he started for the Spanish side of the St. Johns River, his boats carrying a white flag. A few of them landed, and, ascending a hill to the open plain, there fixed the flag on a pole, hoping to draw some of the Spaniards to a conference.

That night fires were seen on the Florida shore, and Oglethorpe suspected the Spaniards were preparing to attack them. In order to gain time to get reenforcements, he had recourse to an ingenious ruse. He had two carriage-guns and two swivel-guns carried to the woods at different points. The

James Oglethorpe

swivel-guns were to fire seven shots, the carriage-guns five, in answer. The smaller guns from the faintness of their report had the sound of a distant ship saluting, the larger that of a battery returning the salute, and completely deceived the enemy. Not until some time after did Oglethorpe know from what danger he had thus escaped. He then learned that the Governor of St. Augustine had arrested his messengers, and had sent picked men with strong boats' crew to attack the fort on St. Simons Island. They had also with them some Yamasee Indians and four guns, hoping, if the settlement was as weak as reported in advices from South Carolina, to dislodge the English.

They were, however, fired upon by the battery at Sea-point, and catching sight of the Hawk in the sound, ran out to sea in greater haste than they had run in. Again they attempted entrance at another inlet, and were in like manner run off by the garrison at St. Andrews, and in such haste that the same night they reached their outposts sixty miles distant.

Holding a conference, their commanders concluded that all the strength of the English was concentrated at St. Simons, hence St. George must be weak, and an attack was determined on for the next night. Fortunately,

Affair With the Spaniards

it was not made, for, from the number of guns they heard, they concluded that reenforcements had arrived. The stratagem had completely deceived them.

That night Oglethorpe had a number of fires made in the woods, and again deceived the Spaniards, who supposed the Creek Indians had come to the aid of the English, and Don Pedro with his command retired behind the walls of St. Augustine. This created consternation in the fort, for the people apprehended that if the Indians should cut off their communication by land, as the sloop of war might do by sea, they would perish by famine. It was under such pressure that the Spanish Governor decided to send back, in the most honorable manner, the two commissioners, and with them an officer of rank to treat with Oglethorpe and request him to restrain the Indians from invading Florida.

Oglethorpe, being ignorant of all this, started to the Spanish side of the St. Johns River, hoping to meet the expected messenger. No messenger appeared, but, instead, a *guarda-costa* with seventy men on board. Oglethorpe had with him only twenty-four men, yet the Spanish fled promptly at sight of them. Afterward two horsemen appeared, and one, apparently an officer, approached

James Oglethorpe

near enough to forbid the English landing on the King of Spain's ground. Oglethorpe courteously replied that he would forbear landing since they objected, but that the Spaniards were welcome to land on the King of England's ground on the opposite side of the river, and should also be welcome to a glass of wine there with himself.

Oglethorpe having received positive information that the Spaniards were supplying themselves with arms and ammunition in Charleston, wrote a letter to the Lieutenant-Governor of South Carolina, requesting him to stop their exportation, and another letter to Mr. Eveleigh, a public-spirited merchant, saying that if the mayor and council could not prevent the sale of arms and ammunition to the Spaniards, then they should buy it all, and thus defeat their plans. He wrote likewise to the Governor of New York.

Strangely enough, the love of gain made many indifferent to the dangers of a sister colony. Spanish gold was filling their treasury; the sight was pleasant; they never looked beyond, where the Spanish soldier, armed with the guns they had furnished, was marching to attack their homes.

Oglethorpe now returned to Fort St. George. He took with him for the relief of

Affair With the Spaniards

the fort Tomo Chichi and his Indians in their canoes, a large periagua, two ten-oared boats with fifty men, cannon, and two months' provisions. On the way he met a boat in which was Mr. Horton, who informed him that two Spanish officers were returning with the commissioners, on a friendly mission to St. Simons. Oglethorpe determined that they should not enter Frederica and thus gain information of its strength and situation. He therefore sent orders for Captain Gascoigne to entertain them on board the Hawk. He also sent a messenger desiring them to anchor, until a safe guard could be sent them, since the country was full of Indians. Indeed, it was fortunate for them that Oglethorpe was an hour ahead of his party, for had the Creeks been foremost, they would certainly have attacked the Spaniards. He could scarcely prevent it, even with an armed boat to escort them to Jekyll Sound.

He went on to Fort George, where he not only gave directions, but worked with the men. He then returned to St. Simons, where he prepared to receive the Spaniards, sent to Darien for some of the most martial-looking Highlanders, ordered marquees and handsome tents to be pitched on Jekyll Island, then announced to the Spaniards that he would wait

James Oglethorpe

upon them next day. To impress the officers that he had cavalry, he went down attended by seven horsemen—all he had. Entering a boat, he approached the Hawk, "whose sailors manned the shrouds, while her marines, with bayonets fixed, lined one side of the deck, and the Highlanders, with drawn broadswords, the other."

CHAPTER XII

WITH THE SPANISH COMMISSIONERS
1736

OF the formal interview on the day following, Oglethorpe gave an accurate account in a letter to the trustees, as follows:

After dinner we drank the King of Britain's and the King of Spain's health, under a discharge of cannon from the ships, which was answered with fifteen pieces of cannon from Delugal's fort at Seapoint. That again was followed by the cannon from St. Andrews, and that by those of Frederica and Darien, as I had ordered. The Spaniards seemed surprised that there should be so many forts, and all within hearing of each other. Don Pedro smiled, and said: "No wonder Don Ignation made more haste home than out." After the healths were done, a great number of Indians came on board, naked, painted, and their heads dressed with feathers. They demanded of me justice against the Spaniards for killing some of their men in time of peace. . . . Don Pedro, having asked several questions, acknowledged himself satisfied of the facts, excusing it by saying he was then in

James Oglethorpe

Mexico, and that the Governor, being newly come from Spain and not knowing the customs of the country, had sent out Indians under the command of Pehoia, King of the Floridas, who had exceeded his orders, which were not to molest the Creeks.

But the Indians not being content with that answer, he promised that on his return to St. Augustine he would have the Pehoia king put to death if he could be taken; and if he could not, that the Spaniards would supply his people with neither powder nor arms nor anything else, but leave them to the Creeks.

The Indians answered that he spake well, and if the Spaniards did what he said, all would be white between them; but if not, they would have revenge, from which, at my desire, they would abstain until a final answer came.

The Indian matters being thus settled, we had a conference with the Spanish commissioners. They thanked me first for restraining the Indians, who were in my power, and hoped I would extend that care to the upper Indians. They then, after having produced their credentials, presented a paper desiring to know by what title I settled upon St. Simons, being lands belonging to the King of Spain. I took the paper, promising an answer next day.

The substance was that the lands belonged to the King of England by undoubted right; that I had proceeded with the utmost caution, having taken with me Indians, the natives and possessors of the lands; that I had examined every place to see

With the Spanish Commissioners

if there were any Spanish possessions, and went forward until I found an outguard of theirs, over against which I settled the English without committing any hostilities, or dislodging any. Therefore I did not extend the King's dominions, but only settled with regular garrisons that part of them which was before a shelter for the Indians, pirates, and such sort of disorderly men.

Oglethorpe, after the departure of the Spaniards, found it necessary to go to Savannah, where all was in commotion. People were bringing complaints against the magistrates, who in turn had their grievances to relate. Oglethorpe went to the court and announced his intentions. "If any one here has been abused or oppressed by any man," he said, "he has free and full liberty of complaining. Let him deliver in his complaints *in writing* at my house. I will read all over myself, and do every particular man justice." Charles Wesley, who was present, reported the complaints so incredible, childish, trifling, that he thought them a full vindication of the magistrates, and was filled with admiration of Oglethorpe's patience in hearing and wise decisions.

No time was ever wasted by this busy Governor, and that night at half past twelve he started for Frederica, but returned to Savan-

James Oglethorpe

nah in ten days to give audience to a party of Creek Indians. At this date we find the resignation of Charles Wesley as secretary. He and Oglethorpe parted as good friends, and he made this record of advice and instruction given him by Oglethorpe just before he sailed for England:

I would you not to let the trustees know your resolution of resigning. There are many hungry fellows ready to catch at the office, and in my absence I can not put in one of my own choosing. The best I can hope for is an honest Presbyterian, as many of the trustees are such. Perhaps they may send me a bad man, and how such an one may influence the traders and obstruct the reception of the Gospel among the heathen you know. I shall be in England before you leave it; then you may either put in a deputy or resign.

On many accounts I should recommend to you marriage, rather than celibacy. You are of a social temper, and would find in the married state the difficulties of working out your own salvation exceedingly lessened, and your helps much increased.

During the following October Oglethorpe concluded a treaty with the Governor of St. Augustine, much more conciliatory than he had anticipated; but his satisfaction at this result was very soon dispelled by the coming of a Spanish envoy from Cuba, who in the name

With the Spanish Commissioners

of his master, the King of Spain, peremptorily demanded that Oglethorpe and his colony evacuate all the territory south of St. Helenas Sound. He would listen to no arguments, but repeated his demands with threats, and unceremoniously departed.

Vigorous measures were now necessary; aid must come from the mother country, or her colony be abandoned. Oglethorpe determined to go at once and represent their condition to the British ministry. The trustees had previously urged his return.

Making the best provision in his power for the defense and local government of his province during his absence, Oglethorpe then set sail for England November 29, 1736. On January 7th Charles Wesley noted in his journal: "The news was brought of Mr. Oglethorpe's arrival. The next day I waited on him, and received a relation of his wonderful deliverance in Bristol Channel. He talked admirably of resignation, and of the impossibility of dying when it is not best."

His reception by the trustees was most cordial, with unanimous vote of thanks for his services. He then made his report—a verbal one—of the progress of their colony, showing the rapid growth of Savannah, of the prosperity of other towns, and the founding of new

James Oglethorpe

ones; of the establishing an important post at Augusta for Indian traffic opened in the interior. He also stated that the Indian tribes to a distance of seven hundred miles acknowledged the King's authority. Yet there was a dark side to this pleasant picture. On the frontiers the colonists were in constant apprehension of invasion from the Spaniards themselves, or their Indian allies, whom they incited to do their utmost against the English. The insolent demands of the Spanish commissioner amounted to a declaration of war, and Oglethorpe urged the necessity of applying to his Majesty for military force sufficient to defend Georgia and South Carolina.

The court of Spain about this time demanded of the English Government the recall of Oglethorpe, evidently considering him a dangerous opponent to their unscrupulous designs. The London Daily Post, in an editorial on the Georgia colony, wrote:

For this reason, it seems, this public-spirited and valuable man is now become the butt of the resentment of Spain, because he has acted like a brave, vigilant, and faithful Englishman, at the expense of his repose and his purse, and to the utmost peril of his life. The Spanish court, we are told, has the modesty to demand from England that he be no longer employed. But I hope the ministers

With the Spanish Commissioners

of Philip V do not think we have a James the First on the throne, or a Gondomar at our court. We have the most undeniable proof that the Spaniards dread the abilities of Mr. Oglethorpe; it is a glorious testimony to his merit and a certificate of his patriotism that ought to endear him to every Briton.

If ever a settlement has been universally applauded by the people of Great Britain, that of Georgia has been so. I happened to be in France when it began, and the uneasiness of the French gave me my first idea of its value. They said the Spaniards neither could nor would suffer it to go on, and from what I both heard and saw, I am persuaded that this late demand concerning Georgia did not take its rise in Madrid. Whatever the Spaniards may pretend, it is France that has the greatest interest in the destruction of that colony. The Indians who are our friends are not only so, but enemies of the French and their Indian allies.

Should we then abandon them, such an impolitic as well as ungenerous and shameful step might in time be attended with fatal consequences not only to the rest of the colonies on the continent of America, but to all future undertakings of like nature. . . . Surely the Queen of Spain does not think we are to be hectored or frightened into measures for making more infant kings! But let her views be what they will, I dare venture to say that our ministers will as soon consent to part with their eyes, as to part with Georgia.

CHAPTER XIII

COMMANDER-IN-CHIEF IN CAROLINA AND GEORGIA
1737–1738

THE next vessel brought important news from America. The Governor of St. Augustine had ordered every English merchant to leave, and was preparing barracks for large numbers of troops expected from Havana. The trustees at once brought before the King a petition asking that a corps be raised for the defense of Georgia. The request was readily granted. His Majesty appointed Oglethorpe general of all his forces in Carolina, as well as Georgia, and commissioned him to raise a regiment. It was thought necessary, however, to send aid to Georgia earlier than the regiment could be completed. The Government arranged to send at once a small body of troops from Gibraltar.

These arrived in Savannah in the spring of the next year. George Whitefield, whom the trustees had engaged to succeed Wesley, sailed with them. About the same time two or three

In Carolina and Georgia

companies of General Oglethorpe's regiment, under command of Lieutenant-Colonel James Cochran, reached Charleston, and from thence marched southward.

The regiment consisted of six companies of one hundred men each. No commissions were sold, but Oglethorpe got such officers appointed as were men of family and character in their respective counties. Twenty young men of no fortune he engaged to serve as cadets, whom he subsequently promoted as vacancies occurred, presenting each with a sum sufficient to provide for an officer's needs. Besides these, he carried with him at his own cost forty supernumeraries. To induce the soldiers to settle in Georgia, every one was permitted to take out a wife, for whose support extra pay and rations were allowed.

At length, all things being ready, Oglethorpe, with six hundred men, women, and children, besides arms, ammunition, and provisions, sailed from Portsmouth in five transports, convoyed by the men-of-war Blandford and Hector. They reached St. Simons Island in a little more than two months, and were received with a salute from the guns of Soldiers Fort and cheers from the garrison. General Oglethorpe encamped with them until suitable arrangements had been made for the comfort

James Oglethorpe

of the troops, then hastened on to Frederica. There magistrates and people joyfully welcomed him. Several Indians also came to greet him, and informed him that the chiefs of every tribe of the Upper and Lower Creeks intended coming so soon as they had notice of his arrival.

Oglethorpe, perceiving at once that a way of communication between the town and the sea forts was a necessity, lost no time in beginning the work. Every male inhabitant was summoned, and, with him, began to cut a road through the woods. So well did the people follow the example of their general that in three days the road was complete—a distance of six miles. It was so well planned that the subsequent safety of the colony was in a large measure secured by this foresight. From the town the road led out in an easterly direction, then, turning south, passed for more than a mile over a fine prairie, thence through a dense forest until it reached a marsh. Along the hard dry margin of the marsh it ran for two miles, bordered on one side by the creeks and swamps, on the other by a close, impenetrable wood matted with vines and palmettos. So narrow was the road that only two men could here walk abreast. From the marsh it passed up to high land, and then in a direct line to the

In Carolina and Georgia

fort. This secured a communication between fort and town. While the forest served for a protection, the narrow causeway made it possible for a few to repel many.

The colonists, especially those of Darien and Frederica, were greatly encouraged by the presence of the general and his troops. For months they had been in constant dread of an attack by the Spaniards, who, notwithstanding their treaty, were greatly increasing the garrison at St. Augustine. They had actually attacked some of the Creek settlements nearest to them, and would have advanced farther had they not been repulsed with much loss. The attack, they pretended, was made by the Florida Indians without their knowledge. The constant alarms had so interfered with the cultivation of the fields that, unless something were done before another harvest, the poorer settlers would suffer. Now, however, all could return to their labor, leaving the defense of their home to abler hands.

There was no time for delay. The first care of the general was to strengthen the frontier posts and distribute his forces for their various duties. Some remained at their forts, some were on the alert for ranging the woods, others made ready for sudden expeditions. Vessels were provided for scouring the sea-

James Oglethorpe

coast and giving notice of the approach of strange shipping. From one place to another the active general passed, not only superintending, but assisting, demanding no comfort of which his men were deprived; indeed, he slept in tents or by watch-fires, while they lay in huts with every reasonable comfort. Harris, writing at the time A Compleat Collection of Voyages and Travels, says: "In all these services, Oglethorpe gave at the same time his orders and his example; there was nothing he did not, that he directed others to do."

Yet even at this early day he had discovered treachery within his camp. He had suspected trouble even on board the Blandford, and had written the trustees:

We have discovered that one of our soldiers has been in the Spanish service, and that he hath strove to induce several men to desert with him on their arrival in Georgia. He designed also to murder the officers, or such persons as could have money, and carry off the plunder. Two of the gang have confessed and accused him, but we can not discover the others. The men were found guilty, and were sentenced to be whipped and drummed out of the regiment. The sequel proved the punishment unwisely lenient, for the ringleader, Shannon, wandered into the Indian districts and endeavored to turn them against the English. Twice he was cap-

In Carolina and Georgia

tured and twice escaped, but finally, with an associate, having murdered two men at Fort Argyle, was taken, tried, and executed, after confessing his crimes.

Up to this time General Oglethorpe had not visited Savannah. He now set out in an open boat, and in two days was received in the town with the firing of cannon, while throngs of people crowded around to bid him welcome. Most of these came because of sincere respect and gratitude to a devoted leader; but there were others who had reason to dread an investigation of their conduct, and would, by loud-mouthed welcome, conciliate his favor. The Governor himself sought to reconcile the discontented and win their esteem. With timely, generous gifts he aided widows and orphans, the sick and all in need. Said one of the citizens: "The general, by his great diligence and at his own expense, has supported things, but we are apprehensive that can not last long, for the expenses are too great for any single man to bear."

It gave Oglethorpe much concern that he had neither time nor funds to encourage improvements. Yet there was some progress. The culture of silk was very limited, yet an Italian family had wound a considerable quan-

James Oglethorpe

tity as fine as any made in Piedmont, and mulberry-trees had increased enough to feed a large stock of worms. Some vines were grown; a potter had discovered clay suitable for making china and had baked some fine specimens of earthenware. A sawmill at Ebenezer turned out daily seven hundred feet of plank. There was cause for encouragement.

Tomo Chichi had been very ill, but on his recovery came to Savannah to see and welcome "the Great Man," as he called Oglethorpe. His joy was unbounded; the sight of his friend made him, he declared, "molt like an eagle," and renewed his health. He asked for an interview for the chiefs of the Creek nations, who were waiting at Yamacraw to come and congratulate Oglethorpe on his return and renew their fidelity to Great Britain. Two days later these chiefs, with thirty of their warriors and fifty attendants, came down the river. They were received with military honors and conducted to the town hall, where the general awaited them. They expressed their satisfaction at once more beholding him, for the Spaniards had persuaded them that he was at St. Augustine, and invited them there to meet him. They went, but finding he was not there, turned back, though offered valuable presents. The Spaniards then said Ogle-

In Carolina and Georgia

thorpe was on board a vessel in their harbor and very ill; they also advised them to break with the English. This they resented, and had now come to assure him of their loyalty and readiness to serve under the general against his enemies. One thousand Creeks would march whenever he commanded.

They reported trouble with Carolina traders, who used false weights and measures, and desired that true ones be lodged with the chiefs of each tribe. This request was at once attended to, and the general also promised, at their earnest invitation, to visit during the next summer their towns, which lay about four hundred miles west of Savannah. Handsome presents were made them, a war-dance held that evening, and in the early morning they set out for their homes.

Oglethorpe himself soon departed, leaving, said one of their number, "many sorrowful countenances and a gloomy prospect of what might ensue." He made only a short stay at Frederica, then proceeded to Cumberland Island and took up his abode at Fort St. Andrews. The troops from Gibraltar, there stationed, had been promised provisions from the King's store for a limited time, and when in November the rations were discontinued, they became dissatisfied.

James Oglethorpe

One day while the general and Captain Mackay were talking, a soldier came forward and unceremoniously demanded their former allowance. Says Stephens in his report: "The general replied that the terms of their enlistment had been fulfilled, and that, if they desired any special favor at his hands, so rude and disrespectful a manner of application was not the way to obtain it. The fellow became outrageously insolent. Captain Mackay drew his sword, which the desperado snatched from his hand, broke in half, and throwing the hilt at the officer's head, ran off to the barracks. There, taking a loaded gun, he cried, 'One and all!' when, followed by five more conspirators, he rushed out and fired at the general. Being only a few paces distant, the ball whizzed close by Oglethorpe's ear, while the powder scorched his face and singed his clothes. Another soldier presented his piece and attempted to discharge it, but fortunately it missed fire. A third then drew his hanger and endeavored to stab the general, who, having by this time unsheathed his sword, parried the thrust, and an officer coming up ran the ruffian through the body. The other frustrated mutineers now tried to escape by flight, but the alarm having spread, they were soon caught and hurried off to jail to await trial."

In Carolina and Georgia

The culprits were sentenced to death, but only the ringleader was executed. However, the spirit of insubordination was quelled, and the southern colonists relieved from all immediate fears.

Early in the spring of that year General Oglethorpe went to Charleston, and, in the presence of the General Assembly of South Carolina, his commission as commander-in-chief of his Majesty's forces was opened and read. Various regulations in the military affairs of that colony were effected, and Oglethorpe returned to his own province. There he spent a busy week among the plantations on the Savannah. To encourage care and industry in the cultivation of their land, he promised for every bushel of Indian corn a bounty of two shillings over and above the market price of the next harvest.

Fearing to give the Spaniards a pretext for hostilities, the trustees had instructed Oglethorpe neither to build new forts nor strengthen the old ones—a needless request, since he had no funds. But, foreseeing that a war between England and either France or Spain (perhaps both) was inevitable, he determined to secure the friendship of the Indians, not so much for the forces they could bring to his aid, but because so long as the

James Oglethorpe

red men were his allies the French would be careful how they weakened their province to support the pretended claims of Spain to Georgia and South Carolina.

CHAPTER XIV

JOURNEYS TO THE INTERIOR
1739

In regard to the necessity of a visit to the Indians in the interior Oglethorpe wrote to the trustees:

I have received frequent and confirmed advices that the Spaniards are striving to bribe the Indians, and particularly the Creek nation, to differ with us; and the disorder of the traders is such as gives but too much room to render the Indians discontented, great numbers of vagrants being gone up without licenses either from Carolina or us. Malachee, the son of the great Brim, called "Emperor of the Creeks" by the Spaniards, and Chigilly, insist upon my coming up to put all things in order; and have acquainted me that all the chiefs of the nation will come down to Coweta town to meet me, and hold there the general assembly of the Indian nations, where they will take such measures as will be necessary to hinder the Spaniards from corrupting and raising sedition among their people.

This journey, though a very fatiguing and dangerous one, is quite necessary to be taken; for if not, the Spaniards, who have sent up great presents to them, will bribe the corrupt part of the nation; and if the honester part is not supported, will probably overcome them and force the whole nation into a war with England. Tomo Chichi and all the Indians advise me to go up. The Coweta town, where the meeting is to be, is nearly five hundred miles from hence. All the towns of the Creeks and of the Cousees and Talapousees, though three hundred miles from the Cowetas, will come down to the meeting. The Choctaws also and the Chickesaws will send thither their deputies; so that seven thousand men depend upon the event of this assembly. The Creeks can furnish fifteen hundred warriors, the Chickesaws five hundred, and the Choctaws five thousand. I am obliged to buy horses and presents to carry up to the meeting.

Early in July Oglethorpe learned that the French had attacked the Lower Creeks and Choctaws, whose settlements joined theirs, and that the Indians were preparing a counter-attack. He determined, therefore, to start at once on his expedition among them, and, if possible, prevent further hostilities. He set out accompanied by Lieutenant Dunbar, Ensign Leman, Mr. Eyre, and his own servants. At the Uchee town, twenty-five miles above Ebenezer, they found saddle and baggage horses, which the general had previously en-

Journeys to the Interior

gaged from the Indian traders. From thence the perilous journey is thus described:

Through tangled thickets, along rough ravines, over dreary swamps in which the horses reared and plunged, the travelers patiently followed their native guides. More than once they had to construct rafts on which to cross the rivers, and many smaller streams were crossed by wading or swimming. . . . Wrapped in his cloak, with his portmanteau for a pillow, their hardy leader lay down to sleep upon the ground, or if the night were wet he sheltered himself in a covert of cypress boughs spread upon poles. For two hundred miles they neither saw a human habitation, nor met a soul; but as they neared their journey's end they found here and there provisions, which the primitive people they were about to visit had deposited for them in the woods. . . . When within fifty miles of his destination, the general was met by a deputation of chiefs who escorted him to Coweta; and although the American aborigines are rarely demonstrative, nothing could exceed the joy manifested by them on Oglethorpe's arrival. . . . By having undertaken so long and difficult a journey for the purpose of visiting them, by coming with only a few attendants in fearless reliance on their good faith, by the readiness with which he accommodated himself to their habits, and by the natural dignity of his deportment, Oglethorpe had won the hearts of his red brothers, whom he was never known to deceive.

James Oglethorpe

On August 11th the chiefs assembled, and the great council was opened with solemn rites. After many "talks," terms of intercourse and stipulations for trading were satisfactorily arranged. Then Oglethorpe, as one of their beloved men, partook with them of the *foskey*, or black-medicine drink—a sacred beverage used only on special occasions, and of which only chiefs, war captains, and beloved men could partake. Afterward they smoked together the calumet, the hallowed pipe of peace. A formal treaty was concluded, by which the Creeks renewed their fealty to the King of Great Britain, and in explicit terms confirmed their grants of territory. The general, in the name of the trustees, "engaged that the English should not encroach upon their reserves, and that the traders should deal fairly and honestly with them."

This last point was the most difficult to settle. "If I had not gone up," wrote Oglethorpe afterward, "the misunderstanding between them and our Carolina traders, fomented by our neighboring nations, would probably have occasioned a war, which I believe might have been the result of this general meeting. But, as their complaints were just and reasonable, I gave them satisfaction in all of them, and everything is settled in peace."

Journeys to the Interior

Not only had the Choctaws agreed not to make war on the French, but the chiefs of all the tribes had assured Oglethorpe that their warriors would march to his assistance whenever he should summon them. We may imagine that the general set out on his homeward journey with a lighter heart, and that his satisfaction was further increased by the congratulations of the trustees, who wrote:

The Carolina people, as well as every one else, must own that no one ever engaged the Indians so strongly in affection as yourself.

Spalding, a more recent writer, speaking of the dangerous journey, says:

When we call to remembrance the force of those tribes, the influence the French had everywhere else obtained over the Indians, the distance he had to travel through solitary pathways exposed to the treachery of every Indian, who knew the rich reward that would have awaited him from Spaniards or French—surely we may ask, What soldier ever gave higher proof of courage? What gentleman ever gave greater evidence of magnanimity? What English governor ever gave such assurance of deep devotion to public duty?

The hardships, mental strain, and anxieties of the expedition too severely taxed the strength of General Oglethorpe. He was

James Oglethorpe

prostrated by fever, and for several weeks was detained in Fort Augusta. While at this outpost on the Savannah he was visited by some chiefs of the Cherokees and Chickasaws, who complained that some of their people had been poisoned by rum bought from the traders, and they threatened revenge. Careful inquiry revealed the facts—unlicensed traders had brought in not only rum, but smallpox. The disease had killed some of the Indians, and the others attributed their deaths to some ingredient in the liquor. With difficulty, Oglethorpe convinced them of the real cause of the sickness, but he assured them that they need not fear traders from Georgia; only licensed ones came, and the strictest precautions were taken before permits were granted.

On his return to Savannah the general met an express messenger from the Lieutenant-Governor of South Carolina, informing him of a serious revolt among the negroes of that province. They had burned several houses and murdered a number of the inhabitants. They had been instigated by a proclamation from the Spanish Governor of St. Augustine, when some slaves had taken refuge there in January. The General Assembly sent a committee to St. Augustine demanding restoration of their property, and, at their request, Ogle-

Journeys to the Interior

thorpe wrote a friendly letter to the Captain-General of Florida to urge their cause in a friendly way. That officer, however, while expressing his friendship for Oglethorpe, exhibited orders to protect all runaway slaves. But after another outbreak in September, General Oglethorpe ordered a troop of rangers to patrol through Georgia and intercept any fugitives; sent Indian runners in pursuit, and directed a detachment from Port Royal to aid the planters of Carolina. He directed the constables to seize all negroes found within Georgia, offering rewards for the captured. At that time it is stated there were forty thousand slaves in South Carolina, and only one-eighth that number of whites, and but for Oglethorpe's prompt action, the colony might have been exterminated.

On October 2d orders were issued that at the beat of the drum on the day following all freeholders of Savannah should be under arms, and at noon the magistrates in their gowns should be in the courthouse. When General Oglethorpe arrived and took his seat the militia, who had been drawn up to receive him, grounded arms and came within. He then made a formal announcement that the English Government had declared war against Spain. Commending the people for their

James Oglethorpe

hearty cheerfulness, he assured them that he had taken every precaution to prevent an enemy coming upon their back from the west or south, and on the seacoast there were English frigates cruising for their protection, while he hoped soon to receive additional land forces. On his return to his lodgings cannon were discharged, and the freeholders with their small arms fired "three handsome volleys."

Nothing escaped the notice of this indefatigable Governor, and in the midst of preparations for war he called a general muster in the interests of peace and good order. The command was that every male inhabitant, including boys, should meet at sunrise to clear the common, public squares, and other places of the shrubs and noxious weeds that spring up so abundantly. They cheerfully responded, and by nightfall had cleared many acres. The general spent the day with them, and every one, without distinction, did what he could. At breakfast he supplied them with bread and beer, and at night they had similar refreshment. He was well pleased with the improved appearance of the space cleared, but there was still another day's work, which he appointed for November 5th, promising a finishing treat and a bonfire. Not only was he gratified with their ready willingness to do

Journeys to the Interior

the work, but he had ascertained accurately what he desired to know—the number of men able to bear arms—an easy and useful method of census-taking.

While in Savannah Oglethorpe lost his valued friend Tomo Chichi. The old man had been "living in wilful poverty, had given away all the rich presents bestowed upon him, always more pleased in giving to others than in possessing himself." He was nearly one hundred years old, yet sensible to the last, peaceful and resigned. He only expressed regret at being called away at this critical time, when he had hoped to be useful to the English in their struggle against the Spaniards.

His devotion to Oglethorpe never wavered. To the last he exhorted his people never to forget the general's kindness, nor the benefits they had received through him from the King. He desired to be buried in Savannah, as he had assisted in founding it. His remains were therefore brought from Yamacraw, and at the landing received by the Governor, magistrates, and the people. The pall was borne by Oglethorpe, Mr. Stephens, and four more gentlemen of the town; Indian mourners followed, and the body was carried to Percival Square, where it was interred with military honors.

CHAPTER XV

TROUBLES IN FLORIDA
1739-1740

OGLETHORPE, being now about to leave Savannah for the southern frontier, made a thorough inspection of the place, its magazines, the arms of the militia; distributed ammunition, and, most difficult task of all, settled difficulties which had come between constables and petty officers, rearranging the whole force and appointing Mr. Stephens to the command. He also granted letters of marque to a seafaring man named Davis, giving him command of a privateer of twenty-four guns, just fitted out at Savannah.

For years the British-American trade had suffered from Spanish *guarda-costas*, which seized merchant vessels, confiscated them, and treated the sailors so cruelly that many died in captivity. The English people demanded redress; a large party severely censured the minister, Sir Robert Walpole, who, as they declared, "tamely saw his country exposed to

Troubles in Florida

such indignities." This minister, knowing the value of peace to a commercial nation, endeavored to settle differences by negotiation. Spain had at last agreed to pay a certain sum of money to make good the losses, while it was agreed that the Governors of Georgia and Florida should refrain from hostilities until boundaries be settled by commissioners from each court. Spain, however, failed to pay the sum agreed upon, and, as we have seen, war had been declared. Admiral Haddock was sent with a powerful fleet to cruise off the Spanish coast; Vernon, with a squadron, to the West Indies; and Oglethorpe ordered to annoy the Spanish settlements in Florida.

In compliance with this order, Oglethorpe had sent for the Indians. He also raised a troop of rangers to prevent the landing of Spanish cavalry, directed the men-of-war to cover the coast, while his regiment protected the islands.

According to the treaty made with the Governor of St. Augustine in 1736, General Oglethorpe had withdrawn the outposts of St. George. Since then the most southern outlook had been on Amelia Island, where he had stationed a scout boat with sixteen men and sergeant's guard, numbering, with their families, about forty persons. The little settlement was

James Oglethorpe

protected with palisades and a battery of several guns. Early in November a party of Spaniards landed at night and hid in the woods. Pistol-shots were heard in the fort; the guard turned out, and soon found the bodies of two Highlanders. They had gone unarmed into the thicket, and had been murdered by the cowardly foe, who escaped to their boats. This outrage occurred just before the writing of the following letter by Oglethorpe to the trustees:

We had not given the least provocation to the Spaniards as yet; but most manfully they have surprised two sick men, cut off their heads, mangled their bodies most barbarously, and as soon as a party and boat appeared, which together did not make their number, retired with the utmost precipitation. A number of scout boats are absolutely necessary. The man-of-war stationed at Charleston can not be here. The launches from St. Augustine can run into almost every inlet in the province; therefore it is absolutely necessary that the trustees should apply to Parliament for at least five ten-oared boats and a troop of rangers. Otherwise there will be no possibility of the people's going out to plant without being murdered as were those Highlanders.

The French have attacked the Carolina Indians, and the Spaniards have invaded us. I wish it may not be resolved between them to root the English

Troubles in Florida

out of America. We here are resolved to die hard, and will not lose one inch of ground without fighting; but we can not do impossibilities. We have no cannon from the King, nor any other guns except some small iron ones bought by the trustees. We have very little powder, no horse for marching, very few boats, and no fund for paying the men but of one boat. The Spaniards have a number of launches, also horse, and a fine train of artillery well provided with all stores.

The best expedient I can think of is to strike first. I am fortifying the town of Frederica, and I hope I shall be paid the expenses—from whom I do not know. Yet I could not think of leaving a number of good houses and merchants' goods, and, what is much more valuable, the lives of men, women, and children, in an open town at the mercy of every party, and the inhabitants either obliged to fly to a fort and leave their property, or suffer with them.

With the Highland Rangers and a select body of Indians, Oglethorpe made an incursion into Florida. At the mouth of the St. Johns River he took and destroyed all their boats, then landing, made a day's march toward St. Augustine. A troop of Spanish cavalry and infantry came out to attack him, but when his Indians raised their war-whoop and advanced, they retreated in most unseemly haste and took shelter in Fort San Diego.

James Oglethorpe

Oglethorpe then retired to the island of St. George, the site of his old fort, and sent Lieutenant Dunbar up the river to destroy all the boats he could find, and thus prevent the Spaniards from crossing into Georgia.

On his return to Frederica he again wrote to the trustees, urging them to send more troops. For want of means he had been forced to call in his Indian allies. They willingly assisted him, but since they thus lost their hunting and corn season, they must be furnished with food and clothing, besides arms and ammunition, which they could otherwise buy with skins they got in hunting. Horsemen he was obliged to have, and had ordered sixty rangers.

I have armed the boats in the cheapest manner [he wrote], with only just enough men to navigate them, and in some saving even this expense. I hope the trustees will represent the necessity of the above expenses to Parliament that the House will grant sufficient to defray them. Or, if Parliament thinks this expense too much for preserving the colony, I hope they will withdraw both the colony and the regiment, since without these necessary defenses they will be exposed to certain destruction.

When General Oglethorpe received from England orders to attack Florida he had at

Troubles in Florida

once notified the Governor of South Carolina, and, having learned that the enemy at St. Augustine was short of provisions, urged the naval commander at Charleston to block the enemy's harbor before supplies could reach them from Cuba. Prompt action was necessary, red tape apparently more so, for the Governor laid the general's letter before the General Assembly; the General Assembly appointed a committee to consider and report the matter; the committee made their report; the report was discussed in both houses; and, at length, it was decided to require General Oglethorpe to explain minutely the nature and extent of the assistance he expected of them! They further "desired to be informed what benefit he conceived *they* might obtain, in case they should grant their aid."

His reply was sufficiently explicit. His principal demand was for 800 pioneers, with tools, provisions, and ammunition. He also advised that they raise a troop of rangers and put them in command of that efficient officer, Captain McPherson, of Darien. Of his own regiment he would take 400 men, leaving the rest for home protection. "Of the people of this province," he wrote, "I can not draft many, because I must not leave the country naked; and if the poor neglect

James Oglethorpe

their planting season it will be difficult for them to subsist; therefore, I would only raise two hundred, which is equal to the number of soldiers I leave behind." He asked also that Carolina contribute a share of the pay of the men, and of rice and corn for the support of their Indian allies.

The St. Johns River had been called by the Indians "Ylacco"; by the Spaniards, "San Matheo o Picolata," or more recently "St. Matthias," and on an expansion of the river they had built a fort which they called St. Francis.

The building of this fort on the north side of St. Matthias River [wrote Oglethorpe] was an absolute infraction of the treaties, and he added:

But it was of great service to St. Augustine, giving an easy means to invade the Creek Indians, or Carolina, and to draw succors from Mexico. They preferred what was useful to what was just, and in defiance of treaties went on with the fortifications.

The Creek Indians greatly desired to take this fort, which was on their lands, and from which the Spanish Indians could easily harass them. Oglethorpe approved, ordered all the boats made ready, and with a detachment of his regiment, the Highland Rangers, and a strong body of Indians and some pieces of cannon, embarked and went up the St. Johns, the Indians going on before. At day-

Troubles in Florida

break on the 7th they surprised and burned the small Fort Picolata, then advanced toward St. Francis. When within musket-shot they opened fire; the Spaniards returned it briskly. While this was going on all day with little effect, Oglethorpe, under the shelter of the wood, was constructing two small batteries. By five o'clock they were ready, when, cutting away the wood which concealed them, he opened fire, and sent to offer terms to the garrison. They at first refused to treat, but at second firing of the cannon, surrendered as prisoners of war. There was in the fort one mortar piece, two carriage and three swivel guns, ammunition, shells, gunpowder, with provisions for two months.

The place being an important one, a garrison was left there under Adjutant Hugh Mackay. Since this fort had been the asylum of runaway negroes from South Carolina, it was hoped that province would do her part in sustaining the place, as well as in laying siege to St. Augustine, for which Mackay wrote: "We want everything, but a willingness in the small number the general has in this colony. If the people of Carolina do their part, or what their allegiance to the King and their own interests ought to induce them to do, we will be masters of St. Augustine before May. But they have acted such a part hitherto that indeed it is not to be expected of them."

Prisoners taken at St. Francis confirmed the reports of scarcity of provisions at St.

James Oglethorpe

Augustine; also that the half galleys had been sent to Havana for supplies, thus leaving the seaboard defenseless. "Such a favorable opportunity must not be lost," said the general, and he sent an express to Carolina, again urging prompt assistance. Again the Assembly deliberated, and requested him to come to Charleston and settle details.

At once he left Frederica, rowed night and day, resting only one hour until he reached his destination, six days after the starting. After many conferences, some plans were agreed upon. Captain Laws was sent to Providence for mortars and powder, letters were despatched to Virginia to have the Hector brought down to the siege, and Captain Warren to block up St. Augustine by sea until the siege should begin.

The Cherokees were already on the march with 500 men, the king of the Chickasaws agreed to come down with all his warriors, and the Creeks with a large number. The Assembly of Carolina failed to send the 800 men promised, but passed an act for raising 400, to be commanded by Colonel Vanderdussen; also a troop of rangers, presents for the Indians, and provisions for three months. General Oglethorpe wrote in regard to Carolina:

Troubles in Florida

This province is very much reduced by sickness, revolts of negroes and other accidents; yet the danger to them from St. Augustine is so great that they agree to raise and maintain a troop of horses and a large body of volunteers for that siege. But their credit being very low and their taxes very heavy, they could not find money for this expense, and I have been obliged to advance them £4,000. I hope that the zeal of the province for his Majesty's service and my poor endeavors will meet with his Majesty's approval.

At length, on May 9th, Oglethorpe, with 400 of his own regiment, the horse and foot rangers he had raised in Georgia, the Creek Indians under Malachee, with Raven, war-chief of the Cherokees, and Tooanahowi, successor of Tomo Chichi, all assembled at St. George Island, at the mouth of the St. Johns. His object being to cut off supplies from St. Augustine, they crossed the river, marched toward the forts, and a body of Indians and light troops attacked San Diego. The fort being defended by several large guns, the first attempt failed. The general came up by this time and, wishing to avoid bloodshed, resorted to stratagem. He had several drums beaten in different parts of the woods, where a few men would appear and suddenly disappear— the same soldiers coming into view at various

James Oglethorpe

localities—until the garrison were convinced that the English general had brought against them overwhelming numbers, and made but faint resistance. When a prisoner, taken at the first attack, was sent to inform them of the kind treatment he and his companions had received, they capitulated.

The Carolina regiment still delayed. Before it arrived Oglethorpe learned that two sloops laden with provisions and ammunition and six Spanish galleys had got into St. Augustine; which might have been prevented had the vessels he asked for arrived in time. It was a grievous disappointment to the anxious general.

On the 18th the Flamborough and the Phœnix anchored in the harbor, reporting also that the Hector and the Squirrel had been left to block the southern entrance to the harbor. The next day General Oglethorpe went on board the Flamborough to hold a conference with Commodore Pearse, and on his return found Colonel Vanderdussen arrived, but without the full complement of his regiment. Orders were issued that all forces advance at once toward St. Augustine. Of that interesting old town and fort Wright says:

> The garrison comprised one hundred cavalry, one hundred artillerymen, detachments from four

Troubles in Florida

regiments, three independent companies, besides local militia, armed negroes, Indians, and convict laborers—altogether 2,000 fighting men. The defenders of castle and town were therefore quite as numerous as all the land force Oglethorpe could bring against them, while their artillery was vastly superior; and any attempt to take the place by land must not only be unsuccessful but cause unnecessary bloodshed, unless a simultaneous movement be made on the water side.

Oglethorpe well understood this, and arranged to march with his land forces as soon as the fleet arrived off the bar in the north channel. A preconcerted signal was to give notice when he was ready to begin the assault, and counter-signal inform him that the ships were ready.

The general began his march. Within three miles of St. Augustine he took Fort Moosa, which had been abandoned by the garrison on his approach. He ordered the gate to be burned and breaches made in the walls, "lest," as he said, "it might one day or other be a mouse-trap for some of our own people." Completing his arrangements, he gave the signal for assault, but, to his surprise, received no counter-signal from the fleet, because, as he learned afterward, "the Spanish galleys were drawn up between the castle and the island,

James Oglethorpe

and any small vessels sent into the channel would be exposed to their fire, as well as that of the batteries, and as no ships of force could follow in support, the party would be defeated, if not wholly destroyed.''

CHAPTER XVI

ATTACK ON THE FLORIDA FORTS
1740

SINCE it had been impossible to take St. Augustine by assault, General Oglethorpe resolved to turn the siege into a blockade. With this intention he returned to Fort Diego and ordered Colonel Palmer, with 100 Highlanders and 140 Indians, to advance, show themselves at Fort Moosa, and scour the woods to cut off communication between St. Augustine and the interior. Colonel Palmer was enjoined to keep strict watch, encamp every night in a different place, avoid coming into action, and return to Fort Diego if a larger force were sent against him. Colonel Vanderdussen with his regiment was to take possession of Point Quartell, about one mile from the castle, and erect a battery commanding the strait, forming the northern entrance to the harbor.

The Spanish battery on Anastasia must be taken before the commodore could send in any vessels. General Oglethorpe, with a part of

James Oglethorpe

his own regiment, some Indians and seamen, undertook to capture the battery, and by skilful maneuvers and quick movement took possession of the sandhills, behind which the enemy had been posted. The Spaniards fled toward their battery, but being closely pressed, rushed into the sea and took refuge in their galleys.

From this place the general determined to bombard St. Augustine. Troops were brought on to the island, all hands employed in constructing new works, and when everything was ready the Spanish Governor was summoned to surrender. To this he replied that he should be happy to shake hands with General Oglethorpe in the castle of St. Augustine. Immediately the batteries were opened and a number of shells thrown into the town, which were returned with vigor, but the distance was too great and little execution was done on either side.

Meanwhile a sad misfortune had befallen the command under Colonel Palmer. That officer was said to be an old Indian officer of great bravery and very little judgment, whose misfortune it was to have a very mean opinion of his enemies. Contrary to his general's orders not to camp more than one night in the same place, he had shut himself up in the

Attack on the Florida Forts

dilapidated old Fort Moosa, and the Spaniards, knowing its defenseless condition, as well as Oglethorpe's absence at Anastatia, sent 600 men to attack the colonel. They made a desperate resistance, but half of them were soon slaughtered, few escaped, and the rest were captured. Colonel Palmer was the first who fell. "The Highlanders fought like lions," said their brave Captain John More McIntosh, who was severely wounded, taken prisoner, and remained long in captivity.

Among the captured was an Indian. The Spaniards delivered him to their Indian allies to be tortured and burned alive. Being apprised of this, Oglethorpe sent a drum with flag of truce and message to the Governor, telling him that if he permitted the burning of the Indian, a Spanish horseman whom he held prisoner should share the same fate. At the same time he wrote asking that this barbarous custom be prohibited, adding that he should be forced to retaliation, and, as they well knew, had more of their prisoners who would suffer than the Spaniards had of theirs.

The Spanish Governor agreed that in future all Indians captured should be treated as prisoners of war. Very often Oglethorpe had to curb the barbarous spirit of his Indian allies. A historian of Florida relates that on

James Oglethorpe

one occasion a Chickasaw having captured a Spaniard, cut off his head and triumphantly brought it to the general, who, instead of rewarding him as he expected, spurned him with abhorrence and drove him from his presence. This Indian, who had lately served the French, indignantly said that a French officer would have rewarded him, and it is added that these Chickasaws showed their dislike for Oglethorpe's humanity by soon deserting him.

For some unknown reason, Commodore Pearse had ordered off the man-of-war stationed outside Matanzas Sound. Consequently several sloops from Havana with provisions and troops entered the channel and reached St. Augustine. That put an end to all hope of starving the garrison, which, from positive information received, was already in distress for want of provisions, and in time a bloodless surrender might have been accomplished.

The general did not yet relinquish his efforts, but decided that while Captain Warren with the fleet attack the half-galleys he would attempt an assault by land. He brought from the island his own regiment, called in the Indians, also the garrison left at Fort Diego, made ready ladders, fascines, etc.—in fact,

Attack on the Florida Forts

provided everything necessary for the assault —then waited for the promised signal from the fleet. He waited in vain. That cautious commander Commodore Pearse, instead of doing his part, calmly sailed away, sending word to the general that it had been resolved to forego the attack, for the hurricane season being at hand, it was deemed imprudent to hazard his Majesty's ships any longer upon the coast!

Never did a commander work against greater difficulties or more harassing disappointments. From Ramsey, in his history of South Carolina, we learn that the troops from that province had proved turbulent and disobedient, that not one was killed by the enemy, though fourteen died from sickness and accidents. Says Stephens: "Most of the gay volunteers ran away in small parties basely and cowardly, as they could get boats to carry them, during the time of greatest need." The greater part of the work had, of course, fallen on the general's regiment and the Georgia companies. These were now so enfeebled by fatigue and heat of the climate that nothing remained but retreat.

The failure to take the Spanish stronghold, like most failures, was not without beneficial results. The most important was that it gave

James Oglethorpe

the Spaniards a wholesome respect for their English enemy, and for a long time kept them on the defensive. The Carolinians were especially relieved in this; indeed, felt none of the effects of active warfare, except on their privateers, until two years later, when in 1742 Georgia was invaded, and then they suffered only from their fears.

General Oglethorpe, encamped on the St. Johns, called on Colonel Vanderdussen for 100 men that he might hold the river and the forts already taken. Not one man could he get. This was especially aggravating, because the general was at that time providing Vanderdussen's men with food, one of the captains of the Carolina regiment having deserted with his company and sailed away in a vessel containing the supplies of the whole corps.

The rest soon followed, Vanderdussen himself passing through Savannah shortly after. In conversation with Mr. Stephens he expressed resentment at the ill conduct of his officers, condemned the cowardly behavior of the runaway volunteers, yet professed himself to be on good terms with the general, of whom he spoke with the greatest deference.

In Charleston Oglethorpe was severely criticised, the newspapers were filled with bitter invectives against him, his whole conduct

Attack on the Florida Forts

was misrepresented, and Vanderdussen made the hero, claiming that he remained with Oglethorpe until the last, entirely overlooking the fact of his failure to make the appointed junction in time, or his refusal to supply the 100 men, and precipitately going home with his regiment. Evidently those Carolinians expected impossibilities, and miles away would direct the conduct of the expedition.

But these were the sentiments of only a portion of the people. All fair-minded citizens of the province condemned not the general, but his calumniators, and spoke of him as the deliverer of the southern provinces of America.

Ramsey excuses the troops of his province by saying:

> The Carolina troops, enfeebled by the heat, despairing of success, and fatigued by fruitless efforts, marched away in large bodies. . . . Many reflections were afterward cast upon General Oglethorpe. He, on the other hand, declared he had no confidence in the provincials, for they refused obedience to his orders and at last abandoned his camp and retreated to Carolina. Grave charges of cowardice, despotism, cruelty, and bribery, made against Oglethorpe in The Plain Dealer of South Carolina, were afterward found to be made by a man who had to leave Georgia to escape trial.

James Oglethorpe

It was the opinion of military men of that day that few generals could have done more than Oglethorpe, and that with only 400 regular soldiers the wonder was that his small force was not destroyed by an enemy secure in a strong castle well garrisoned. The Duke of Argyle spoke on this subject before the House of Peers, and with no uncertain sound:

One man there is, my lords, whose natural generosity, contempt of danger, and regard for the public prompted him to obviate the designs of the Spaniards and to attack them in their own territories; a man whom, by long acquaintance, I can confidently affirm to have been equal to the undertaking, and to have learned the art of war by a regular education, who yet miscarried in the design only for want of supplies necessary to a possibility of success.

CHAPTER XVII

PEACE AND THE COMING OF WHITEFIELD
1740

ON the same date Oglethorpe wrote from Frederica to the Under-Secretary, Andrew Stone, Esq.:

It is necessary for me to make several expenses to preserve this province, particularly fortifying. For this I must draw upon England. You will see the estimate among my papers. Necessity of protecting the province will force me to finish entrenchments around this place. It would be a sad thing to have a province abandoned and the people, at least the improvements, destroyed. If I can complete the Rangers and the Highland Foot again and man the armed sloops, boats, and schooners, I do not doubt to keep the province, notwithstanding what the Governor of St. Augustine says in his intercepted letter. I must beg you in proper season to drop a word for my reimbursement. I would not trouble you only I know your good inclination to favor those who sacrifice their interests for the public safety, and do not desire you to speak at any season but when it will be agreeable.

James Oglethorpe

Peace seems now to have smiled upon the province for a brief time, a time industriously used by the Governor for the improvement of his colony, and especially of Frederica, then a small town of 1,000 inhabitants. He had designed the place for a military post; therefore, instead of the regular squares, parks, gardens, broad shade streets, with which he had beautified Savannah, there was an esplanade and parade-ground, and everything for the defense of a frontier town. South of the fort the streets were about forty feet wide, and the houses all built of brick or of tabby, the best and cheapest material for his purpose. This tabby is a compound of lime, sand, shells or pebbles, mixed with water, a most durable material, resisting for ages the action of the elements. It is about the same as the coquina used in the walls and buildings of St. Augustine, and still seen in the ruins. In Spain walls of the same substance have endured for centuries.

On the island of St. Simons, besides the town of Frederica, was a small village called Little St. Simons, also Soldiers Fort, both at the southern end of the island. A road had been built connecting Frederica with the fort. For a mile it led through a beautiful prairie, then entered the forest, and just here Ogle-

Peace and White field

thorpe had established his unpretending home —a simple cottage, with garden and orchard of oranges, figs, grapes, and other fruits. The house was shaded by evergreen oaks and commanded a view of the town and fortifications, as well as the sound. Here he could enjoy a quiet retreat, watch the progress of the defenses, and at a moment's warning be ready for service.

Many of his officers lived near, some in far more pretentious dwellings. Captain Raymond Demeré, a Huguenot of fortune, spent large sums upon his country-seat, which was built after the French style and enclosed with hedges of orange and cassina plants. Thomas Spalding, when describing the home of Oglethorpe, states that, after the general went to England, it became the property of the Spalding family; that during the Revolutionary War the buildings were destroyed, and that his father afterward sold the property. The fine oaks remained standing until within a few years.

That Oglethorpe did not acquire or claim any land in Georgia beyond this small home, or receive any in return for his services, is proved by a letter from General Washington, written five years after Oglethorpe's death, in reply to one from a French nobleman claiming

James Oglethorpe

to be his descendant. After saying that careful inquiry had been made and that there were no lands in Georgia belonging to Oglethorpe, Washington adds:

If there had been property of that gentleman in Georgia, in the time of the late war with Great Britain, so far from it having been confiscated, it would have met with singular protection in consequence of the high estimation in which the character of General Oglethorpe stood in that State.

Frederica stood on a high bluff on the west side of the island. Its streets were named after the officers in Oglethorpe's regiment; on its north side was their camp, on the east their parade-ground, and on the south a small forest, which concealed them from an enemy coming up on the water side. On Jekyll Island were defensive works; on Cumberland Island a battery; another at Fort William. "Seldom," says Wright, "has one with such limited means more forcibly evinced his power. Not only Georgia, but Carolina owed their preservation to the ability shown in the disposition of these works, for, as it has been observed, St. Simons was destined to become the Thermopylæ of the southern Anglo-American provinces."

It was during this interval of peace from Spanish depredations that the Rev. George

Peace and Whitefield

Whitefield visited Georgia, remained a few months, then returned to England to be ordained, and to collect funds to found in Georgia an orphanage. He had come to the Georgia colony as their missionary, had been presented by the trustees with the living of Savannah, and had obtained from them a grant of five hundred acres for the support of the destitute orphan children of the province.

Mr. Whitefield made himself famous in England, not only by the fervor of his piety, but by his fearless, if sometimes unwise, rebukes, especially of the clergy. On his return to America all classes flocked to hear him preach. He spoke with great severity of the ministers of that day, calling them "dumb dogs," "slothful shepherds," and avowed his firm belief that few of the doctors of an age or more past could ever enter heaven. An Episcopal clergyman, the Rev. Alexander Gordon, retorted with equal bitterness, pointing out the pernicious tendency of Whitefield's words and doctrines, called him a religious quack, and, preaching against him, used the text: "Those that have turned the world upside down, are come hither also." Whitefield replied from the words of Paul: "Alexander the coppersmith did me much evil, the Lord reward him according to his works."

James Oglethorpe

Other ministers suffered his rebukes, and their friends stirred up to their defense. That was not all, for, like his predecessor, he made the mistake of considering the pulpit a sphere too limited, and went into the court-room to harangue the jury. Even in Frederica, Oglethorpe's peace was disturbed by reports of the commotion in Savannah.

Whitefield had begun the building of the orphanage on a sandy bluff near Savannah. Disputes soon arose between him and those who had orphans in charge. Mr. Parker, one of the magistrates, had with him two boys whom Whitefield claimed. The elder boy was sixteen, and Parker refused to give him up, saying he had maintained him in childhood and it was unfair to take him, now that he could be of some service. To which the preacher said: "The boy is so much fitter for my purpose; he can be employed for the benefit of the orphans."

The result was that Parker lost his temper, and Whitefield gained his point, carrying off both boys. Oglethorpe was appealed to, and thought that Whitefield had gone beyond the intention of the trustees in taking strong boys, old enough to be serviceable to the colony, particularly during the planting season; and he finally had to interfere with the dictatorial

GEORGE WHITEFIELD.

Peace and Whitefield

ways of the determined minister. Three orphan children by the name of Mellidge had shown themselves so intelligent and industrious that Oglethorpe had encouraged the eldest, John, to do what he could in the way of planting, while the sister kept the house and took care of the younger brother. The latter Whitefield removed to the orphanage in spite of the protests of their brother John.

The boy complained to Oglethorpe, then at Frederica, and an answer was received by Mr. Noble Jones to this effect:

As for the Mellidge brothers, I think your representation is very just; that taking them away to the Orphan-house will break up a family which is in a likely way of living comfortably. Mr. Whitefield's design is for the good of the people and the glory of God; and I dare say when he considers this, he will be very well satisfied with the return of the two younger children to their brother, John Mellidge, since they can assist him. Upon this head I am to acquaint you that I have inspected the grant relating to the Orphan-house. Mr. Seward said that the Trustees had granted the orphans to Mr. Whitefield, but I showed him it could not be in the sense he seemed to understand it. It is most certain that the orphans are human creatures, and neither cattle nor any other kind of chattels; therefore can not be granted.

But the Trustees have granted the *care* of the

James Oglethorpe

helpless orphans to Mr. Whitefield, and have given him five hundred acres of land, and a power of collecting charities, as a consideration for maintaining all the orphans who are in necessity in this Province; and thereby the Trustees think themselves discharged from maintaining any. But at the same time, the trustees have not given, as I see, any power to Mr. Whitefield to receive the effects of orphans, much less to take by force any orphans who can maintain themselves, or whom any substantial person will maintain. The Trustees, in this, act according to the law of England: In case orphans are left destitute they become the charge of the parish, and the parish may put them out to be taken care of; but if any person will maintain them, so that they are not chargeable to the parish, then the parish does not meddle with them.

On receipt of this letter John Mellidge was advised to inform Mr. Whitefield of General Oglethorpe's opinion, and ask permission to take his brother and sister home. Whitefield's answer was: "Your brother and sister are at their proper home already; I know no other home they have to go to. Give my service to the general, and tell him so." Receiving this message, Oglethorpe promptly ordered Mr. Jones to take the children away from the orphan-house. Mr. Whitefield complained that he had been badly treated, and threatened

Peace and Whitefield

to appeal to the Trustees, but there the matter ended. John Mellidge showed himself worthy of the charge of his brother and sister, and became afterward Representative from Savannah in the first General Assembly of Georgia.

Whitefield's ideas about the management of the orphans were peculiar, and the orphanage, according to his own description, a dismal place. The mornings were spent in school, the afternoons in something useful; no time was set apart for play, because he considered all such time as "Satan's darling hours to tempt children to all manner of wickedness." So that, although there came to be seventy children in his orphan family, he boasted that "there was no more noise than if it were a private house."

However mistaken Whitefield may have been in regard to the needs of child-life, he intended and believed that he was bringing up those children to the glory of God. Undoubtedly his work was a great blessing, and as such was acknowledged by General Oglethorpe. Apparently he was in advance of his day. A letter printed in the London Magazine in 1745 says:

It gave me much satisfaction to have an opportunity to see this Orphan-house, as the design has made such a noise in Europe; and the very being

James Oglethorpe

of such a place was so much doubted everywhere, that even no farther from it than New England, affidavits were made to the contrary.

Whitefield being much of the time absent, the management of the orphanage was entrusted to his friend, James Habersham, who complained of the arbitrary conduct of the magistrates. Having become prejudiced against the founder of the institution, they did injustice to the institution itself by withdrawing from it students who promised to become ornaments to society and binding them out as servants. Habersham's remonstrances were treated with contempt. General Oglethorpe at first refused to interfere; but that he did on some occasions is seen from the following letter to him by Whitefield:

August 18, 1742.

HONORED SIR: I most heartily thank you for being so kind to my family in Georgia and for espousing my friends' cause when I think they were wronged. In a letter I yesterday laid the case before the Honorable Trustees, not doubting but they will preserve us from oppression and from persecution in all shapes. I think we have only the glory of God and the good of the colony at heart. Prejudices may be raised against us by evil reports and misrepresentations, but your Excellency is more noble than to hearken to insinuations which

Peace and Whitefield

are not supported by evident matter of fact. I am sure God will bless you for defending the cause of the fatherless, and espousing the cause of injured innocence. My friends will, I trust, at all times readily acknowledge anything they may either say or do wrong; and if I know anything of my own heart, I would not offend any one causelessly or willfully for the world. In a few months I hope to see Georgia. In the meanwhile I beg your Excellency to accept these few lines of thanks from, honored sir, your Excellency's

Most obliged and humble servant,
GEORGE WHITEFIELD.

Whitefield returned to Georgia, and his life and work there became more peaceful. Oglethorpe esteemed him highly, and when, on September 30, 1770, he died, there was profound sorrow in Savannah. Church and Statehouse were draped in black, and the Governor and his council put on mourning. By his will Whitefield left the orphan-house to "that elect lady, that mother in Israel, the Right Honorable Selina, Countess Dowager of Huntingdon."

In the spring of 1740 the British ministry resolved to "annoy Spain in her American possessions." In November the King assured Parliament that he meant to prosecute the war vigorously, even though France espoused the Spanish cause. But, before war was declared,

James Oglethorpe

the French, in violation of treaties, had sailed in conjunction with the Spanish to the West Indies and threatened Jamaica. Admiral Vernon, with a powerful fleet, was sent in January to oppose them, but, instead of going to Havana, turned toward Hispaniola in order to watch the French fleet, thus losing time and an opportunity to attack Havana under favorable circumstances. A letter from Oglethorpe, written at the time to the Duke of Newcastle, gives a formal account of the condition of affairs. It is dated in May, 1741:

MY LORD: Since my last I have sent out a party of Creek Indians under command of one of their war captains, Accouclauh. Two of our scout boats landed them in the night in Florida; they marched up to Augustine and took one of their horsemen prisoner, and beat a party of their horse. I send the prisoner by Captain Thompson to your Grace, that his Majesty may have an exact account of the condition of St. Augustine. What he says is confirmed by other advices; that they have eight hundred men newly arrived, six hundred of them regular troops. Besides what he says, my intelligence mentions that Admiral Vernon and the troops from England are employed in the West Indies, and can not come up to attack the Havannah, and that as soon as the Governor of Havannah sees the effect of the expedition, they will send up more

Peace and Whitefield

troops and half-galleys for the attacking this province and South Carolina. My private intelligence further adds that Spanish emissaries have been employed to fire the English towns and magazines of North America, and to take other measures to hinder the supplying this great English expedition with provisions.

I send your Grace enclosed our present strength. If our numbers were but equal, and the men-of-war would but stop their communication, we might still take the place, for our Indians keep them blocked up. But if our men-of-war will not keep them from coming in by sea, and we have no succor, but decrease daily by different accidents, all we can do will be to die bravely in his Majesty's service.

I must therefore entreat your Grace to move his Majesty that there be a train of artillery, arms, and ammunition sent over; also orders for completing our two troops of Rangers to sixty men each, the Highlanders to one hundred, and one hundred boatmen; with orders to buy or build and man two half-galleys.

I have often desired assistance of the men-of-war, and continue to do so. I go on fortifying this town, making magazines, and doing everything I can to defend the Province vigorously. I hope my endeavors will be approved of by his Majesty, since the whole end of my life is to do the duty of a faithful servant and grateful subject.

I have thirty Spanish prisoners in this place, and we continue so masters of Florida that the

James Oglethorpe

Spaniards have not been able to rebuild any one of the *seven forts which we destroyed* in the last expedition.

Permit me with the greatest humility to return my most grateful thanks to his Majesty and to your Grace for the company and officers added to this regiment, and at the same time desire your Grace to move his Majesty in the matters above mentioned, which, in my opinion, are absolutely necessary for the preservation of this Province.

CHAPTER XVIII

WAR WITH THE SPANIARDS AGAIN
1741

GENERAL OGLETHORPE'S letter was laid before the "lords justices," who approved all save the application for artillery and military stores, which they referred to the master-general of ordnance. The master-general of ordnance referred it to his principal officers to report upon. The officers summoned Mr. Verelst for details; Mr. Verelst could not furnish the details, did not know whether the 600 swords called for were wanted for regiment, militia, or Indians. The laws of red tape required just that particular piece of information; hence, delay number one.

The second delay came from the very natural conceit of the officers, who firmly believed that they knew more of Georgia than Oglethorpe did, and decided that the ordnance he asked for was too heavy. "We are very well informed," said they in their report, "that all the Continent for one hundred miles

James Oglethorpe

and upward is a sheer sand, and that they have no materials to support the works, so that we can not think of sending any ordnance heavier than a twelve-pounder for the use of the forts.''

There was still a third and longer delay, when the demand for half-galleys was referred to the Admiralty. Half a dozen meetings, with due intervals between for ponderous reflection, were given to the subject before any decision was reached.

Meantime, Oglethorpe was again forced to appeal to the Home Government. He was supplied with flour either from England or the northern colonies. Of late Spanish privateers had been making prizes of these merchant vessels, having taken one off Charleston with 1,500 pounds of goods on board. Only two men-of-war being stationed on the coast, they were not able to defend both Charleston and Frederica. After hearing of the last capture, Oglethorpe ordered out the guard-sloop with a detachment from his regiment, and hired a schooner belonging to Captain Davis. These two vessels met with three Spanish half-galleys, and having forced them to fly, then overtook and attacked one of their privateers, which they drove ashore and disabled. This, however, was not only expensive,

War with the Spaniards Again

but dangerous; Oglethorpe therefore bought a suitable vessel and fitted it out for service. He excused the purchase by saying the loss to English shipping, with their cargoes, etc., would be far greater than the cost of the vessel, not to speak of the distress of the colony for want of provisions.

On August 16th a large Spanish ship was seen off the bar of Jekyll Sound. General Oglethorpe being notified, took the guard-sloop, also the sloop Falcon and the schooner Norfolk, with some of his own regiment, and started in pursuit. A violent storm arose, and when it was over the ship had disappeared. The Falcon had been disabled by the storm, and had to put back, but with the other two Oglethorpe sailed direct for Florida, and on the 21st descried, five leagues distant, the Spanish vessel at anchor. There was a dead calm, but he ordered out the boats, which towed them along until they came up to the enemy, a Spanish man-of-war and the Black Sloop, a notorious privateer. Oglethorpe, whose courage seemed equal to any occasion, gave orders for boarding. His vessels bore down upon the Spaniards, who opened fire, which was so vigorously returned that they weighed anchor, and a light breeze having sprung up, speedily ran over the bar. The

James Oglethorpe

English followed and, though they did not succeed in boarding, engaged them for an hour, when the Spaniards sailed for the town, so disabled that six half-galleys came out to cover their retreat, keeping, however, at a safe distance. Three or four Spanish ships were lying in the harbor, but none ventured to attack the plucky little Georgia vessels, and that night Oglethorpe lay at anchor within sight of St. Augustine. For some days he cruised off the bar, and then, having alarmed the whole Spanish coast, returned to Frederica.

With a spirit like this, Oglethorpe and his brave, enduring men, had they been supplied with what he had asked, could soon have intimidated the Spaniards and put an end to the war. The expenses gave him much uneasiness, though he had freely used his private fortune in the cause so dear to his heart.

For some years Oglethorpe had been corresponding with Governor Clark, of New York, and with him laboring to accomplish a noble object. In writing to the trustees, Oglethorpe speaks of that object as:

Most advantageous to all the British settlements in America—which is, to make peace between all Indians under the British crown, and thereby prevent their destroying each other as they do now.

War with the Spaniards Again

Besides the saving of so many lives and making the western parts safe, it would enable the English Indians to act with more vigor and greater numbers against the Spanish or any nation at war with us. The men who would be otherwise forced to stay at home for their own defense will be enabled to leave their towns by the peace.

I have with much difficulty made a peace between the Chickasaws, Cherokees, and Creeks; but the great work of making a peace between them and the Six Nations remains with Governor Clark to do. If the Chickasaws can obtain a peace with the Six Nations, which are called the Black Enemy, they will be secured against the French. The Black Enemy did prevent their coming down this year to war against the Spaniards, whereas last year they sent down forty men, and if peace is made with the Six Nations, they will send down every year two hundred. The Cherokees have acquainted me that if they are secured from the Black Enemy, who lately killed their emperor, Moy Toy, they will be able to furnish me two thousand men. . . . As the treaty is of greater consequence to Georgia than to any other colony, I drew for £100 sterling on Mr. Verelst toward defraying the charges, which I hope you will reimburse.''

The trustees approved the course. Whether the funds were furnished is another question to be settled later. Not one of all the colonial leaders had ever exercised so good an influence

James Oglethorpe

over the native tribes as Oglethorpe, nor had any other been so well able to control them. The humane, unselfish motives which governed all his movements in the founding of his colony seemed to have impressed the savage and secured his friendship. Lord Baltimore and William Penn had been successful in obtaining from the Indians large grants of land; they had wisely adopted the best methods of getting peaceable possessions and retaining large estates. Penn's were securely flanked on either side by Virginia and Maryland. With Oglethorpe the case was different. He induced the savages to cede to him a large province, but not one acre for himself; his work was wholly for others, and with trying embarrassments. The weak and factious Carolinians failed to do even their simple duty in self-defense; the long-established colonies of France and Spain were bitter enemies, and it was largely due to the fidelity of his Indian allies that he was able to preserve the colony he had founded. "If we had no other evidence of the great abilities of Oglethorpe," says Spalding, "but what is offered by the devotion of the Indian tribes to him and to his memory afterward for fifty years, it is all sufficient, for only master minds acquire this deep and lasting influence over other men."

War with the Spaniards Again

Oglethorpe complained often of his want of sure and direct correspondence with England. "Seven out of eight letters miscarry," said he, and from December to April he had no safe opportunity of sending letters. In that year, 1742, he reported no vessels taken by the Spanish privateers. His spirited attack on their man-of-war and privateer had made them more than cautious. With two guard-vessels he again started for St. Augustine, but a storm came up so violent that with great difficulty he saved his ships. Several English vessels were lost; another would have gone down but for his timely aid. Just at this time a privateer arrived off the bar at St. Augustine, with flour, clothing, and supplies for that garrison. A pilot had been sent with two half-galleys and 200 men to convoy her in. The Governor had received the announcement of her arrival with great satisfaction, had ordered the guns fired, and sent a party of Indians to cut wood and make a bonfire.

Oglethorpe's Indians attacked them and took five prisoners, while Captain Dunbar with his guard-ship came up with the Spanish vessel before it was high water, captured her, and took her to Frederica. This prize Oglethorpe detained some months for the service of the colony. A Charleston merchant wrote: "Our

James Oglethorpe

wrongheads now begin to own that the security of our Southern settlements and trade is owing to the vigilance and unwearied endeavors of his Excellency in annoying the enemy." Oglethorpe had sent to St. Augustine a number of prisoners in exchange for some Carolina marines. These had brought the same reports as had the Indian spies, to which the general refers in his letter to the Duke of Newcastle, June 7, 1742:

The Indian spies bring me word that the Spaniards have received powerful succor; that all their houses are filled with new soldiers, and that their common talk is bragging that they intend to attack us and overrun all North America. They are some of the troops which were raised for the defense of Cuba. I hope your Grace will remember that I long ago acquainted you that I anticipated an invasion as soon as the affair with Cuba was ended, and prayed for succors, which are not yet arrived. The Spaniards have, as I then believed, sent more troops, and expect a general revolt of the negroes. It is too late now to ask your Grace to represent this to his Majesty and ask succors. Before they arrive the matter will be over. I hope I shall behave as well as one with as few men and as little artillery can. I have great advantage from my knowledge of the country, and the soldiers and inhabitants are in good heart and used to fatigue and arms. We have often seen and drove the

War with the Spaniards Again

Spaniards, and I believe that one of us is as good as ten of them. I hope your Grace will represent the situation, for though the present affair will be over before any succor can come, yet, if we defeat the enemy, it will facilitate our taking St. Augustine if troops arrive; and if none come, our succors will only secure our own.

In another letter of the same date, Oglethorpe says of the Spanish efforts to excite a revolt among the negroes of Carolina:

They won't pass by us into Carolina, so must take us in their way, and I believe they will meet with a morsel not easy to be digested. Yet we are not in the situation we would wish, being very weak in cannon and shot, never having had any from England, nor indeed anything else since my last arrival in this country, but one store ship of powder and small arms from his Grace the Duke of Argyle just before he was out of ordnance. From the time he quitted the service until now I have been left to shift for myself. I have sent northward to raise men and to buy guns and ammunition of all kinds, and have, according to standing orders, drawn bills for his Majesty's service with orders to Mr. Verelst to apply thereupon to the Treasury.

A few days previous to the writing of this letter Oglethorpe had sent Captain Hamer of the Flamborough against some vessels going from Havana to St. Augustine with reenforce-

James Oglethorpe

ments. A storm had separated ten of those vessels from the rest of the fleet; these Captain Hamer attacked and drove some ashore, but in so doing lost a score of his men and one boat. He returned to notify the general; then, instead of remaining to guard the coast, sailed back to Charleston. A despatch was sent to the Lieutenant-Governor of South Carolina informing him of the arrival of several vessels at St. Augustine, but Governor Bull's only reply was that he was well assured that it was only the annual relief sent from Havana, that the same vessels carried back a like number of men. Further advices of fifteen more strange vessels in sight failed to convince him, nor could the general purchase from him the various military stores needed. He "seemed to take no notice," nor was the naval commander, Maxwell, more successful. Captain Frankland promised, it is true, to send two vessels, but failed to keep the promise. This indifference of the Lieutenant-Governor brought forth a plain letter from the general. Among other advice, he said:

> You would be right to have the militia immediately reviewed and ready for service. I expect the Spaniards to attack us, and if they do, doubt not to give them a warm reception and make them sick of it; but if they should get the better of us, they

War with the Spaniards Again

will immediately follow their advantage, and you may expect a visit, and it is possible that they may incite an insurrection among the negroes. I expect you to send to Fort Frederic what is necessary for the defense of that place, of which I send you an estimate and one to the Assembly to be laid before them. If there is any trifling in this, and an accident thereupon should happen, you are answerable for it. I have often given notice how the place was neglected. Some of the men in the garrison were countenanced in their desertion, and harbored by some ill-designed people. I therefore desire you should publish a proclamation for the apprehending of them, setting forth the consequences to those who receive them. These men have been four years in the regiment and never attempted to desert till in garrison in the province of Carolina.

The letter had no effect. Governor Bull paid no attention to the advice of the "Commander-in-Chief of his Majesty's forces in Georgia and Carolina." The ruling faction of Charleston, with Bull at their head, resolved to defend themselves on their own ground, refused to send to Georgia any further assistance, and planters in the exposed districts fled to Charleston with their families. From the Gentleman's Magazine, of London, this deserved criticism is taken:

The Lieutenant-Governor therefore prepared for war by appointing a long train of aides-de-camp.

James Oglethorpe

He at the same time nominated Mr. Vanderdussen captain-general and commander-in-chief by land and sea, and created numberless officers of rank from general down to captain. The militia were mustered and reviewed, dilapidated batteries were repaired, rusty guns were remounted, and the Spaniards being still two hundred miles off, a most martial spirit was displayed by these men, who left the true defender of their province, as well as his own, to stand or fall, as the case might be, before a vastly superior force.

General Oglethorpe had at no time taken counsel of his fears, and in this case his apprehensions were but too well founded. Before the month had passed a Spanish fleet of above fifty vessels, with between 5,000 and 6,000 soldiers on board, were ordered to attack the colonies. Fourteen vessels attempted to run in at Fort William, but were driven off by guns from the fort, aided by the guard-schooner under Captain Dunbar, and they then entered Cumberland Sound. General Oglethorpe immediately ordered out a detachment and some Indians under Captain Horton, while he followed with a part of his regiment in three boats. "He was at once attacked by the enemy, but with two boats fought his way through the whole fleet. The third boat, under Lieutenant Tolson, ran into a creek, lay con-

War with the Spaniards Again

cealed until next day, then returned to St. Simons and reported the general overpowered and killed. But Oglethorpe, by keeping to the leeward and thus taking advantage of the smoke, escaped in safety, while the Spaniards had suffered so much in the engagement that four of their vessels foundered on their way back to St. Augustine for repairs. The officer in command at Frederica had watched the engagement from the masthead, and seeing the general surrounded by the enemy, concluded he was lost, and at once sent despatches to Charleston for immediate assistance. Their joy was unbounded when, on the following day, their commander returned unhurt."

He now withdrew the garrison from St. Andrews, on the north end of the island, to reenforce Fort William, laid an embargo on all vessels in the harbor, took into service the merchant ship Success, and called in from Darien the Highland companies, of whom he said: "They are, next to the Indians, the most useful in those grounds where regular troops can not form." He also withdrew from various outposts the Rangers, gave presents to the Indians, rewarded those who did extraordinary duty, and promised promotion to all who should distinguish themselves.

His undaunted active spirit inspired his

James Oglethorpe

soldiers. "We were ready for twice our number of Spaniards," said the crew of the Success, which had twenty guns and 100 men. Besides the Success, there were in this harbor "the general's schooner of fourteen guns, St. Philip's sloop of fourteen guns, and eight York sloops close inshore, with one man on board each to sink or run them on shore in case of being overpowered."

The conflict soon came. On July 5th *thirty-six* Spanish vessels ran into St. Simons harbor in line of battle. They were received with a brisk fire from the forts and from the shipping. Three times they attempted to board the Success, but each time failed, and after an engagement of four hours gave it up and sailed up the river toward Frederica.

Oglethorpe ordered his own men ashore, and, thanking the seamen for their brave resistance, directed the vessels to make their way out of the harbor as best they could. This they did, and soon reached Charleston in safety. During this engagement General Oglethorpe had been not only on shipboard and at the batteries, but acted as engineer, since Colonel Cook, whose duty it was, had, on hearing of the invasion, retired to Charleston; and, as if that were too near the scene

War with the Spaniards Again

of action, hastened to England, followed by the subengineer, his son-in-law.

A council of war was called. It was decided to destroy batteries, provisions, etc., at St. Simons, and retire to Frederica. This was speedily accomplished, and that evening the invaders landed and took possession of the abandoned camp. From several prisoners taken by the Indians the general learned that the enemy had land forces of 5,000 men who had orders to *give no quarter*. Mr. Rutledge, of Charleston, wrote afterward to the Under-Secretary:

The Spaniards were resolved to put all to the sword, not to spare a life, so as to terrify the English from any future thought of resettling. Said a prisoner from on board: "During the time they lay off this bar, the Spaniards whetted their swords and held their knives to this deponent's and other English prisoners' throats, saying they would cut the throats of all those they should take in Georgia."

Never had the young colony been in such danger, and never had the general so much need of help, which was still withheld. Yet he calmly faced the multiplying dangers, happily increasing the confidence of his people, and stirring up his soldiers with a like determination to resist the invaders to the last.

James Oglethorpe

Detachments of Spaniards sought to invest the fort, attempting to pass through the wood, but were driven back by the watchful Indians. The only avenue to Frederica was by the road so wisely planned some time previous—the forest on one side, marsh on the other, and so narrow that only three men could walk abreast. Neither artillery nor baggage could be taken over it, and the Spanish troops who ventured were so harassed by the Highlanders and Indians who lay in ambush that their attempts ended in serious loss. They, however, succeeded, after many trials, in approaching within two miles of the town.

Wishing to encounter the enemy before they reached the open ground, Oglethorpe led a body of Highlanders, Rangers, and Indians and charged so fiercely that all but a few were either killed or taken prisoners. He captured two with his own hands, and the Spanish commander was taken by a ranger. Another Spanish officer shot the Indian Tooanahowi in his right arm, but the savage drew his pistol with his left hand and killed the officer on the spot. For more than a mile they pursued them, and then halted to await the regulars. These Oglethorpe posted to guard the pass, and returned to the town to prepare the company of marines and encourage the people.

War with the Spaniards Again

Meanwhile the Spanish again advanced, halting where, unsuspected, the English lay in ambush. They had built their fires and were making ready their kettles for cooking when a horse took fright and startled them. They ran for their arms, but were shot down by the invisible enemy. Their principal officers were killed, and the men fled in confusion, throwing away their muskets and leaving their equipage on the field. Don Antonio Barba was mortally wounded. The Spaniards regarded the loss of this commander as worse than a thousand men. A Spanish sergeant declared, "The woods were so full of Indians that the devil himself could not get through them." So great was the slaughter that the place was long known as "Bloody Marsh." The general with his men marched over the causeway to within two miles of the Spanish encampment, intercepting all who had been dispersed in the late fight, and there he passed the night.

The invaders retired within the ruins of St. Simons Fort, and began entrenching themselves where they would be under the protection of their ships. Finding it unwise to attack them, Oglethorpe went back to Frederica to refresh his wearied soldiers, and to send out parties of rangers and Indians to harass the enemy and watch their motions. He now ap-

James Oglethorpe

pointed his staff: Lieutenants Maxwell and Mackay as aides-de-camp, Lieutenant Sutherland brigade-major, and at the same time promoted Sergeant Stuart to be ensign, in reward for bravery in the late engagement.

No help still from Carolina nor the men-of-war. Their stock of provisions was neither good nor abundant, for some had been burned rather than leave them for the enemy, and, with their vessels blocking the sound, no more could be brought in. All this gave the general the greatest anxiety, yet it must be carefully concealed from his brave little army, which, all told, numbered only 800 men.

The people who remained in Frederica were assured that, if the worst came, they had a safe retreat through Alligators Creek and the canal cut through Generals Island, whence they could go to Savannah. The soldiers were encouraged to patient endurance by seeing their general undergoing every privation to which they were exposed. Changing their tactics, the Spaniards now proceeded up the river with their galleys, but were again prevented from landing by the Indians concealed among the tall grass and shrubs. Going on toward the town, the galleys were received with so determined a fire from the batteries that they retreated in haste to the shelter of their ships.

War with the Spaniards Again

Thus was defeated the villainous plot of a Spanish officer, who had surrendered and been taken prisoner but refused to be exchanged, pretending that his countrymen looked upon him as a traitor. Permission had been given him to go to some northern colony, and a boat furnished to convey him to Darien; but in a few days he returned, saying he could not risk being captured. The general was still unsuspecting, but just at this time an English prisoner escaped from the Spanish commodore's ship, declared that he had seen the man, and heard him planning to return to Frederica, and when the galleys attacked the town, he would fire the arsenal, and in the confusion the assault would be a success. The man's conduct since his return had been suspicious, and he was now closely confined; so his plot was a failure.

Several more escaped prisoners came in, and all agreed in the report that the Spaniards, not expecting such desperate resistance, were much dispirited. There were numbers of wounded and sick in distressing conditions. There was much dissension, and the Cuban forces had separated from those of Florida. Oglethorpe meditated a surprise, had marched to within a mile of the Spaniards, and was about to make the attack when a Frenchman,

James Oglethorpe

who without his knowledge had come down with the volunteers, being a spy, fired his gun and deserted, and was not overtaken.

Knowing that the spy would expose his weakness, Oglethorpe determined by a little stratagem to make him appear a double spy and thus frustrate his schemes. He therefore hired a prisoner to carry a letter to the deserter. "The letter was in French," said Oglethorpe, when relating the affair, "as if from a friend, telling him that he had received the money, and would strive to make the Spaniards believe the English were very weak; that he should undertake to pilot their boats and galleys, and then bring them into the woods where the hidden batteries were. That if he could bring about all this, he should have double the reward, and that the French deserters should have all that had been promised them.

"The Spanish prisoner got into their camp," continued Oglethorpe, "and was immediately carried before the general. He was asked how he escaped and whether he had any letters; but denying this, was searched and the letter found. And he, upon being pardoned, confessed that he had received money to carry it to the Frenchman, for the letter was not directed. The Frenchman, of course, denied knowing anything of the contents of the letter,

War with the Spaniards Again

or having received any money or had any correspondence with me. Notwithstanding which, a council of war was held and they decided the Frenchman a double spy, but the general would not suffer him to be executed, having been employed by himself."

The Spaniards were sadly perplexed, and, while deliberating, some English vessels appeared off the coast, thus apparently confirming a statement of the letter, that "six or seven men-of-war" were coming to their assistance. They decided to leave at once, and their fears increasing as the moments passed, they burned the barracks at St. Simons, and so hastily re-embarked that they left behind their great cannon, a quantity of ammunition and provisions, and those dead of their wounds unburied. In the meantime three or four large vessels had been seen off the north end of the island, and Oglethorpe, certainly expecting they were coming to his aid, sent Lieutenant Maxwell in a boat with a letter to the commanding officer.

The lieutenant found no vessels in sight. It was afterward learned that one was the Flamborough, and that when Captain Hamer was asked why he sailed away at so critical a time, replied that his orders were "to come and see if the Spanish fleet had possession of the

James Oglethorpe

fort, and, if they had, to return immediately to Carolina!" Fortunately the safety of Frederica did not depend on the assistance rendered by a sister colony whose officers seemed afraid to look a Spaniard in the face.

By this time some of the invaders had put out to sea; others, landing at St. Andrews, camped for the night. Two days after twenty-eight vessels entered the harbor of Fort William and demanded the surrender of the garrison. But Ensign Stuart, having received promise of aid from General Oglethorpe, replied that he would not yield the fort, nor could they take it. Those who attempted to land were suddenly fired upon by rangers, who had, by forced marches, just arrived, and were concealed behind the sand hills. The galleys tried to batter the fort with their cannon, but were soon disabled by the few eighteen-pounders of the fort. After an assault of three hours, the Spaniards gave up and retired to St. Augustine.

Again several English vessels were seen off St. Simons, and again they sailed away, replying to the commander-in-chief's summons that the orders from the Lieutenant-Governor of South Carolina were to return with the vessels in case the Spaniards were gone; and Captain Hardy added that for his part he should go in

War with the Spaniards Again

search of a prize with the rest of the King's ships.

Thus with *two* ships and *800* men had Oglethorpe defeated an enemy having *fifty-six* ships and above *5,000* men. Says Wright:

Not only was the infant colony delivered from a formidable foe, but the people of South Carolina were saved from the horrors of a servile war such as that from which they had previously suffered, and that by a man whom they had persecuted and calumniated because he would not permit their traders to cheat the Indians and poison them with rum.

"The deliverance of Georgia from the Spaniards," wrote Whitefield, "is such as can not be paralleled but by some instances out of the Old Testament. The Spaniards had intended to attack Carolina, but wanting water, they put into Georgia, and so would take that colony on their way. They were wonderfully repelled, and sent away before our ships were seen."

The Governors of New York, New Jersey, Pennsylvania, Maryland, Virginia, and North Carolina wrote to Oglethorpe thanking him for his invaluable services to the Carolinas, and expressing their gratitude to God that he had placed the destinies of the southern colonies under the direction of one so well qualified for the important trust.

It was the misfortune of South Carolina to

James Oglethorpe

be at that time under the rule of Governor Bull and his faction. The majority of their honorable people heartily condemned his policy, and united with the people of Port Royal in their letter to General Oglethorpe, saying: "If the Spaniards had succeeded in their attempts, they would have destroyed us, laid our province waste and desolate, and filled our habitations with blood and slaughter. . . . We are very sensible of the great protection and safety we have long enjoyed by having your Excellency to the southward of us; had you been cut off, we must, of course, have fallen."

CHAPTER XIX

AFTER THE WAR
1742-1743

GENERAL OGLETHORPE did not share the belief that the Spanish war was over. In his report, while rejoicing over the present deliverance, he wrote:

I have sent all hands to work on the fortifications. have sent northward to raise men for another battalion, have sent for cannon, shot, etc., for provisions and all kinds of stores, since I expect the enemy, who (though greatly terrified) lost but few men in comparison to their numbers, as soon as they have recovered from their fright, will attack us again with more caution and better discipline.

I hope his Majesty will approve the measures I have taken, and that he will be graciously pleased to order troops, artillery, and other necessaries sufficient for the defense of this frontier and the neighboring provinces; and I do not doubt with a moderate support, not only to be able to defend these provinces, but also to dislodge the enemy from St. Augustine.

After the War

The following months brought new anxieties and new disappointments to General Oglethorpe. Captain Frankland, with a fleet of twelve vessels, arrived in August, and Oglethorpe joined him with ardent hopes of engaging the enemy and putting them to flight. But, with strange weakness, the captain refused to allow his vessels to venture over the bar of St. Augustine, and his ships returned to their various stations.

Again, a detachment of 500 men from Jamaica arrived in Charleston with orders to return if the Spaniards no longer threatened British territory. Their colonel was informed by Governor Bull that the southern colonies were perfectly safe and there was no necessity for him to proceed with his men to Georgia. In reference to this affair a gentleman of South Carolina wrote indignantly:

> This self-sufficiency of ours is well known to General Oglethorpe, who no doubt has been beforehand with me in animadverting upon it. . . . The general, in answer to a letter received, with that of the colonel, expressed himself with a good deal of warmth upon our not thinking ourselves in immediate danger, and to the colonel he answered that in his opinion the King's service required that the detachment should come to Frederica; but that since the people of this province did not apprehend

James Oglethorpe

immediate danger, he could not take it upon himself to give positive orders; the colonel should do what appeared most agreeable to his instructions from General Wentworth.

In reality the colonies were far from safety, as will be seen from a letter of Oglethorpe to the secretary, in which he informs him of the killing of a party of Rangers by Spanish troops, and of the burning of Mount Venture by the Yamasee Spanish Indians. Authentic information had also been received of large reenforcements arrived at St. Augustine; that the Spanish were determined to have revenge for their late defeat and losses, and their plan was to have the French make an attack along the Savannah River, while they would capture Frederica.

Oglethorpe again appealed to the home Government. "I shall do all I can," he wrote, "to balk their expectations. It was with much difficulty, and not without the apparent hand of God, that we made head this last time against a vastly superior force, and that with a very few cannon. Doubtless they are stronger now, and will take better measures; but we have no addition, and the men-of-war have refused to stay in the port."

After the War

On the same day the general wrote to the secretary complaining of the "stupidity, not to say worse," of the Carolinians in preventing the men-of-war from coming to his aid; for, said he, "the Spaniards intend, if they succeed in taking Georgia, to push their conquests as far as Virginia; all North and South Carolina are full of provisions, and a very busy Spanish faction is stirring at Charleston."

Reading this, and much more showing the lethargy and indifference toward the fate of their colony across the sea, we are not surprised when a biographer of Oglethorpe recalls the remark of Oxenstiern: "See, my son, with how little wisdom nations are governed." The English Government was as slow in rewarding its soldiers as it was their general. The prize sloop captured by Captain Dunbar, and now sent over to be valued and the amount given to captain and crew for gallant service, was for "many months" unnoticed, though Captain Dunbar "begged for an answer, as she was badly wanted in the colony." The long delay damaged the cargo, so that very little remained for the captors.

In the spring of this year, 1743, we find General Oglethorpe again in camp on the St.

James Oglethorpe

Johns. The Spaniards, having been largely reenforced, had repulsed successfully all Indians sent against them, and a strong force was marching toward the St. Johns. The general resolved to attack them before they were joined by troops from Cuba, already on the way.

His first attempt was successful. His Indians advanced undiscovered, and before daylight killed forty men, with the loss of only one on their side, and forced the enemy to retire within their walls. No efforts would induce them to make another advance at that time. "I did all I could to draw them into action," wrote Oglethorpe, "and having posted troops in ambuscade, advanced myself, with very few men, in sight of the town, intending to skirmish and retire in order to draw them into the ambuscade; but they were so meek that there was no provoking them."

"The Spaniards bearing all these insults gives our Indians a very contemptible notion of them," wrote an officer from the camp. "The general encourages this contempt, though he at the same time believes it no want of courage in the Spaniards, but that they wait to provoke him to some rash action, or to engage on disadvantageous ground, which, notwithstanding the general's

After the War

vivacity, he seems always cautious to beware of. It is also probable that they may have orders not to hazard anything in small actions, but to keep their troops entire until the arrival of the armament from Cuba."

Oglethorpe's schooner and the Success were cruising off the Florida coast. The general sometimes joined them. While sailing up the channel to reconnoiter St. Augustine he came near being killed by the bursting of a gun on board. He was so severely hurt that the blood gushed from his nose and ears, but he soon recovered to reassure his horrified men.

Failing to draw out the Spanish, Oglethorpe returned to Frederica with his Indians, whose devotion and prompt response to his summons were a great satisfaction, and in unhappy contrast to the attitude of some Carolinians, who still withheld their support. Andrew Rutledge, Esq., of Charleston, and Chief Justice of South Carolina, was not among that class. He wrote of those Indians: "They are much charmed with his Excellency's noble conduct, and their adherence to the English is now too well established for even the nonsense of this place to remove or weaken. This late motion of his has done an inconceivable service to our quiet here for

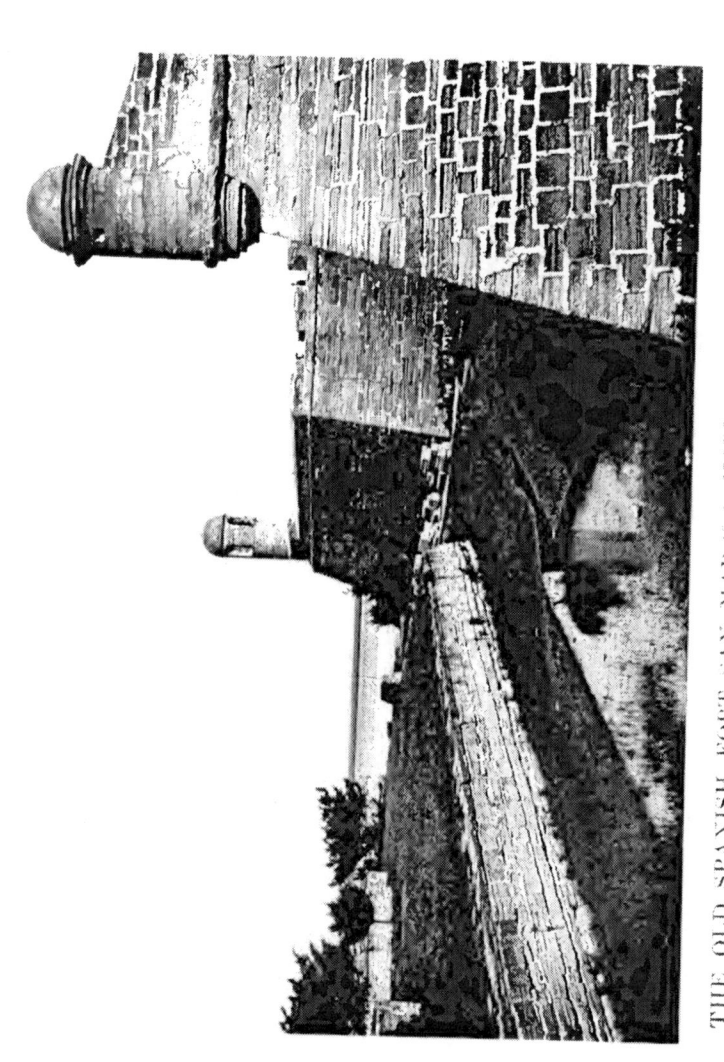

THE OLD SPANISH FORT SAN MARCOS, NOW CALLED FORT MARION, ST. AUGUSTINE, FLORIDA.

COPYRIGHT, 1901, BY DETROIT PHOTOGRAPHIC CO.

James Oglethorpe

the present, though we murmur because *he* was the actor; for the majority of this town like nothing more than to lay hold on all occasions to villify the man to whom they owe their protection."

Human nature was the same then as now, and we have no doubt Captain Dunbar was correct when he concluded "that what were thought to be the sentiments of that province was no more than the voice of Charleston factors, who for their commissions bartered the effects of British merchants with planters for their crops, and who would never put the welfare of their country in competition with their profit in trade."

That the conduct of the Governor of South Carolina proceeded from ignorance, as Oglethorpe suggested, is more than doubtful. He could scarcely have pursued a course more deliberately dangerous than that recounted in the next letter from Oglethorpe himself, who says:

The Spaniards are now preparing for an expedition from Havannah. In their late invasion of this province, one of our chief advantages lay in their want of pilots and guides. The Governor of St. Augustine has sent to Charleston a Spanish vessel to exchange prisoners, many of whom are pilots by water or guides by land. Lieutenant-Governor

After the War

Bull suffered this vessel, which was commanded by one of the Spaniards' best pilots, to go over, and consequently learn the bar of that town, and ventured to receive a message from his Majesty's enemies, without acquainting the general who commands in chief his Majesty's forces in that province. He also received Alexander Paris, who piloted the Spaniards into St. Simons harbor, and who now walks about Charleston in full liberty. . . .

These pilots may be of the greatest advantage to the Spaniards in the ensuing expedition, if designed against us, since it lays our harbors open and makes the fastnesses of our woods less advantageous. . . .

Very soon Oglethorpe forwarded to England documents, sworn and proved, which revealed the fact that *not only provisions, but ammunition, were delivered in St. Augustine by vessels from Charleston!*

The Spaniards made every effort to seduce the Indians from their allegiance to the English, but in vain. Similli, a Creek chief, went into St. Augustine, as he said, "to know what they were doing." The Spaniards there offered him large sums of money for every English prisoner he would bring in; showed him fine scarlet clothes and a sword which they had presented to the captain of the Yamasees, saying of Oglethorpe: "He is poor, he can give you nothing; it is foolish for you to go back to him."

James Oglethorpe

The Creek answered: "We love him. It is true he does not give us silver, but he gives us everything we want that he has. He has given me the coat off his back and the blanket from under him." Then they quarreled with him, struck him with a sword, leaving a scar which he showed after his escape.

CHAPTER XX

RETURN TO ENGLAND—THE PRETENDER
1743

AMONG the colonial records of this date is a letter from Captain George Dunbar to the Duke of Newcastle. In this letter Captain Dunbar says that he had been instructed by General Oglethorpe to ask leave for him to come home "at such a time as he should find it necessary for the king's service to lay before his Majesty the situation of that country." There was then imperative necessity for Oglethorpe's going to England. "His pecuniary resources were dried up, and bills which he had drawn for his Majesty's service to the amount of £12,000 had been returned dishonored!" He put the frontier in the best possible state of defense, appointed Mr. Stephens Deputy Governor of Savannah, and that efficient officer Major Horton military commander of Frederica. On July 23, 1743, he embarked in the Success for England.

In the memoir of General Lachlin McIn-

Return to England

tosh, of Revolutionary fame, is related an incident occurring just before General Oglethorpe left Georgia. It will be remembered that in 1740 that gallant captain John Moore McIntosh had been taken captive. He was for four months confined in St. Augustine, then in Havana for three months, when he was taken to St. Sebastian, in old Spain, and confined in the common jail, with no allowance but bread and water. The year following he was released, but died soon after, leaving two sons, William and Lachlin. Oglethorpe attached the two young men to his regiment, and in due time obtained for them commissions. They heard of an uprising in their native Highlands, and determined to return to Scotland and enlist under the Pretender. They concealed themselves in the hold of the vessel, but were discovered, and before the vessel sailed were brought before Oglethorpe, who was on board.

He reminded them of his esteem for their father, and sought to persuade them of their folly and the hopelessness of every attempt of the Stuarts. The boys appeared to be unconvinced. He then informed them that it would be his duty to put them under arrest, but added: "Assure me you will think no more of your wild project; keep your own

James Oglethorpe

secret, and I shall forget all that has passed between us." The boys were now subdued, promised to follow his advice, and were sent on shore, never again to see the face of their benefactor. One of them became in after-years brigadier-general of the Revolutionary army, and related to his biographer this story of his last interview with General Oglethorpe.

We might now expect to find a record of thanks from Parliament to the man who had rendered his country such unselfish, able service. No such record appears, although Admiral Vernon, who had perhaps taken better care of himself than of his country on this occasion, received a vote of thanks from that discriminating body. Nor could Oglethorpe retire to his country-seat, at Godalming, a laurel-crowned hero. His estates were encumbered by liabilities incurred in the public service, which a tardy Parliament failed to acknowledge, though the Lords Justices not only passed the accounts, but sanctioned an additional outlay of £8,000 a year.

Yet nothing was done during that session of Parliament. For fifteen months it went on, until, to the great relief of his faithful agents, Oglethorpe reached England, September 28, 1743. Enemies from Charleston had

Return to England

arrived before him. He had long ago been informed of the intrigues which Colonel Cooke, chief engineer of his own regiment, and Vanderdussen, hero of the Carolina faction, were carrying on against him. He had wasted neither time nor thought on their venomous attacks—the defense of two colonies he had ever placed before his own interests—but having discharged those higher duties, he was now ready to refute their slanders.

Alexander Vanderdussen was a disreputable Dutchman, driven from his own country for criminal conduct; afterward employed by the Spaniards in the Philippine Islands, from whence he carried off a wealthy lady for her effects and settled in South Carolina. This man the General Assembly of that colony had selected to lead a regiment to Oglethorpe's assistance. He failed to render the general any efficient aid, but was wily enough to make it appear so, and became the hero of the day, while all failures were attributed to Oglethorpe. Notwithstanding his protests of fidelity to his commander, he joined in the accusations of Colonel Cooke—the invalid colonel, who scented danger from afar and retired under pretense of illness, first to Charleston, then to England, to recruit his

James Oglethorpe

health. He owed all his promotion to General Oglethorpe, but gratitude was not among his virtues, and he presented *nineteen* articles against the moral and military character of his patron.

A board of officers sat for two days examining the charges, article after article, and the witnesses on both sides. At the conclusion the officers unanimously pronounced the whole accusation, "*in each and all of its articles, false, malicious, and groundless.*" The board made a report of the same to his Majesty, also adding several facts proved against Colonel Cooke, and the King ordered that officer dismissed from the service.

Meantime, amid his embarrassments, Oglethorpe remembered his colony across the seas and continued to make urgent appeals in their behalf. Reports from Major Horton were gratifying to the anxious general. While they were daily expecting an invasion from the Spaniards, they were of good courage, in good health, the men all at their posts and determined not to give up the colony but with their lives. The young province was learning the lesson of self-reliance and self-support. The mother country seemed to have thrown them off; neither do we find any intimation that Oglethorpe was ever repaid the

Return to England

large amounts expended from his private means in this public service.

The year 1744 was an eventful one to Oglethorpe. In March he had been selected as one of the general officers appointed to oppose the threatened invasion of France; in May he was on the committee of the Foundling Hospital; in September his marriage occurred—an event only surprising because so long delayed. He was fifty-five when united to Elizabeth, only child and heiress of Sir Nathan Wright, Bart., of Cranham Hall, Essex. It is with satisfaction that we learn, in regard to this union, "the evening of their lives was tranquil and pleasant after a stormy noon."

The manor in the village of Cranham was henceforth their home. Here for forty years the general retired when not in service, and enjoyed the rural occupations in which he took delight. The old mansion no longer exists; the only structures that yet remain of that old home are the walls of the extensive gardens. "These walls, beyond which was a fosse, being about twelve feet high and two feet thick, are strongly built of red brick, and loopholed; while the gates, likewise unimpaired except by time, are fine specimens of workmanship in wrought iron."

James Oglethorpe

Mrs. Oglethorpe's fortune greatly relieved the financial embarrassment of her husband, for it was many years before his own estates were free from the heavy burdens his services in Georgia had left upon them. In 1745 Oglethorpe was promoted to the rank of major-general, and owing to home troubles in the rebellion of the "Young Pretender," was detained in England by order of the Government. From his colony he heard that the Indians still continued faithful, and were looking for his return; that the Spaniards had made no further advances, but were abundantly supplied with provisions from New York and South Carolina. Oglethorpe raised some recruits for the Georgia Rangers, but when the Success, with the men and supplies on board, was ready for sea, she was ordered to Hull instead.

Oglethorpe, with other troops, was sent to join the Duke of Cumberland, and in three days the newly raised forces marched over snow and ice more than one hundred miles. The duke gave orders for immediate pursuit of the rebels. For four days they continued this, with hot skirmishing on both sides. The weather was fearful, the troops exhausted, but surely gaining on the retreating enemy, until at last the Young Pretender

Return to England

realized his case was hopeless, and with his deluded followers departed for Scotland.

The Duke of Cumberland returned to London with flying colors and as much applause as if the rebellion had been completely quelled. During the short struggle General Oglethorpe had several times remonstrated with the royal duke for allowing cruelties on the adherents of the Pretender. Though willing and anxious to crush the rebellion, he refused to be a party to any barbarity, or even injustice, and thus incurred the displeasure of the duke, who had him arraigned before a military tribunal for having "lingered on the road."

Oglethorpe was duly tried and "honorably acquitted" by a court-martial of eight generals and brigadiers and seven colonels. The Gazette of the day announced this, adding: "His Majesty was pleased to confirm the verdict." Oglethorpe had now attained the rank of lieutenant-general. He regularly attended the sessions of Parliament, speaking occasionally upon some bill to relieve distress or correct abuses. In behalf of the Moravians, or United Brethren, he made a long and impressive argument, tracing their origin and history and giving the constitution of their Church, bearing testimony to their pious

James Oglethorpe

and useful labors in the colonies. "A bill to the desired effect having passed the Commons, was carried by sixteen members to the House of Lords, where Oglethorpe, as their spokesman, delivered it to Lord Chancellor Hardwicke. The bill was approved by their lordships, and received the royal assent."

In this, as in other measures for the good of the soldiers, Oglethorpe was in the minority. He was often in advance of his time. His high sense of justice and honor did not always meet with a happy or heartfelt response. His plain talk of the duty of Parliament grew monotonous, and perhaps more than one member echoed the sentiments of Walpole, who said of him: "It was very certain that he was a troublesome and tiresome speaker, though even that was now and then tempered with sense."

It was fortunate for the colony of Georgia, and a source of great satisfaction to Oglethorpe, that he could leave at the head of affairs brave and true men—men who not only governed their own province with discretion, but afterward rendered essential service during the war of the Revolution. They may even be said to have taken part in the battle of Bunker Hill, for it is related that "Joseph Habersham, Noble Jones, and a few others

Return to England

broke open the king's magazine at Savannah, took from it 500 pounds of powder and sent it to Boston, where it was used in the battle of Bunker Hill."

When, a little later, two British men-of-war appeared at Tybee, near Savannah, the "Council of Safety" met and, without a dissenting voice, resolved to burn their homes rather than allow them to fall into the hands of the British. So long as Oglethorpe had continued with the colony he opposed and prevented the introduction of negro slaves. After his departure various influences united to favor their coming. England had always urged it; the climate, the English thought, called for the negro laborer.

Bancroft tells us that so good and upright a man as Whitefield "believed that God's providence would certainly make slavery terminate to the good of the Africans, and he pleaded before the trustees in its favor, as essential to the good of Georgia." The opposition of the Moravians was quieted by this message from Germany: "If you take slaves in faith, and with the intent of conducting them to Christ, the action will not be a sin, and may prove a benediction."

The Hon. James Habersham, friend of Whitefield, provincial secretary, and acknowl-

James Oglethorpe

edged to be "one of the sweetest, purest, most useful, and noblest characters in the long line of colonial worthies," counseled the introduction of slaves. Oglethorpe and the trustees had often received petitions to have slaves brought in, but had always refused to listen to such requests, pointing to the neighboring colony, where slaves had brought the people to the brink of ruin. The Salzburgers and Highlanders had refused to sign such petitions, and drew up a counter one, giving good reasons against the bringing in of slaves, especially the nearness of the Spaniards (who proclaimed freedom to all slaves who ran from their masters) and the wrong to the negro. "For our own sakes, our wives, our children, and our posterity," they concluded, "we protest against it." The majority prevailed. The negroes were at first hired from their owners in South Carolina, and finally purchased from them and the northern colonies.

CHAPTER XXI

OLD AGE AND DEATH
1754-1785

OGLETHORPE's public career ended in 1754, when he and his colleague failed to be returned from Haslemere, the borough they had so long represented in Parliament. Henceforth his life was retired, and not much is known concerning him. Occasionally we hear of him in the literary circles of that day. The sympathies which attracted him to Oliver Goldsmith are easily recognized in the following letter:

How just, sir, were your observations that the poorest objects were by extreme poverty deprived of the benefit of hospitals erected for the relief of the poorest! Extreme poverty, which should be the strongest recommendation to charity, is here the insurmountable objection, which leaves the distressed to perish. The qualifying such persons to receive the benefits of hospitals answers the intentions of the intended society. The design is the immediate relief from perishing, thereby giving time and protection to get proper destinations, and the

James Oglethorpe

being admitted into a hospital is the proper destination. You were so good as to offer to distribute such sums as should be sent you. At the same time that I am to return you thanks for your charitable offer, I am to send you five pounds to distribute for that purpose, in the time and manner you think proper. Which I accordingly herewith send. . . .

If a farm and a mere country scene will be a little refreshment from the smoke of London, we shall be glad of the happiness of seeing you at Cranham Hall. It is sixteen miles from the Three Nuns at Whitechapel, where Prior, our stage-coach, inns. He sets out at two in the afternoon. I am, sir,

Your obedient humble servant,

J. OGLETHORPE.

CRANHAM HALL.

On April 13, 1773, Dr. Samuel Johnson, Goldsmith, and Boswell dined with Oglethorpe at his town house, and while the latter did not join in a discussion between the two doctors, he much enjoyed at the close a song from Goldsmith, "to a pretty Irish tune, The Humors of Bellamagairy."

Just one year later they met again with Oglethorpe. Goldsmith had died, but there joined them Mr. Langston and the Irish Dr. Campbell. It was on this occasion that Dr. Johnson urged Oglethorpe to give the world his Life. Dr. Campbell states that Ogle-

SAMUEL JOHNSON.

Old Age and Death

thorpe "excused himself, saying that the life of a private man was not worthy of public notice," and seemed also to excuse himself on the score of incapacity. Yet he asked Boswell to bring him some good almanac that he might recollect dates; whereupon Boswell said he need only furnish the skeleton, and that Dr. Johnson would supply bones and sinews. "He would be a good doctor who could do that," retorted Oglethorpe. "Well," said Campbell, "he is a good doctor," at which Johnson laughed very heartily.

The American Revolution had now begun, and one of our historians, Mr. Hugh McCall, states that the British offered to General Oglethorpe command of the forces sent to subdue the colonists, but that he refused to accept the position unless the ministry would authorize him to assure the colonists that justice should be done them; apparently a reasonable request, yet Oglethorpe remained in England.

There appears to be some doubt about the authenticity of this story; especially is it improbable when one remembers that Oglethorpe was then in his eighty-eighth year. But we have no reason to doubt his declaration, "that he knew the people of America well; that they could never be subdued by

James Oglethorpe

arms, but their obedience could ever be secured by treating them justly."

Holmes, in his Annals of America, gives an incident occurring at the close of the war: A day or two after John Adams arrived in London as ambassador from the United States he was waited upon by Oglethorpe, who politely introduced himself and said:

"I am come to pay my respects to the first American ambassador and his family, whom I am very glad to see in England." He then wrote Mr. Adams, expressed his great regard for America, much regret at the misunderstanding between the two countries, and added that he was happy to have lived to see the termination of it. Mr. Adams returned the visit and had another interview of an hour or two, but failed to report anything further.

In the year 1783 Horace Walpole wrote to the Countess of Ossary that he had just made the acquaintance of one a little his senior; that they were to be intimate a long time, for his new friend was but ninety-four! The new friend was Oglethorpe, whom he had not seen for twenty years, yet knew him instantly. "As he did not recollect me," says Walpole, "I told him it was a proof how little he was altered, and I how much. I said

Old Age and Death

I would visit him; he replied, 'No, no; I can walk better than you. I will come to you.'"

Later on, the same writer spoke of Oglethorpe as having the activity of youth compared with himself, who was twenty years younger, and declared that "Oglethorpe's eyes, ears, articulation, limbs, and memory would suit a boy, if a boy could recollect a century backward. His teeth are gone, he is a shadow, and a wrinkled one; but his spirits and his spirit are in full bloom." This was from the man who never admired him, and who, after Oglethorpe's death, wrote again to the countess:

I make no commentary on General Oglethorpe's death, madam, because his very long life was the curiosity, and the moment he is dead the rarity is over; and as he was but ninety-seven he will not be a prodigy compared to those who reached to a century and a half. He is like many who make a noise in their own time from some singularity which is forgotten when it comes to be registered with others of the same genius, but more extraordinary of their kind. How little will Dr. Johnson be remembered when confounded with the mass of authors of his own caliber!

We need not be surprised at these remarkable sentiments coming from one who, if he

James Oglethorpe

always spoke of Oglethorpe as a "bully," denominated George Washington "an excellent fanfaron," and seemed, as Macaulay observed, "never to have formed a single friendship." Very different was the estimate placed upon him by Burke, who once remarked that he looked upon Oglethorpe as a more extraordinary person than any he had ever read of, for he founded a province and lived to see it severed from the empire which created it, and become an independent state. Hannah More, describing him when he was above ninety, writes to her sister:

> I have got a new admirer, and we flirt together prodigiously; it is the famous General Oglethorpe, perhaps the most remarkable man of his time. He is above ninety years old, and the finest figure of a man I ever saw. He perfectly realizes my ideas of Nestor. His literature is great, his knowledge of the world extensive, and his faculties as bright as ever. He is one of the three persons still living who were mentioned by Pope. Lord Mansfield and Lord Marchmont are the other two. He was the intimate friend of Southern, the tragic poet, and all the wits of his time. I went to see him the other day and he would have entertained me by repeating passages from Sir Eldred (her first work). He is quite a *preux chevalier*, heroic, romantic, and full of the old gallantry.

Old Age and Death

The poets Thompson and Pope sang his praises, and Dr. Wharton, who knew him well, quoting Pope's famous couplet,

> One driven by strong benevolence of soul,
> Shall fly like Oglethorpe from pole to pole,

said: "Here are lines that will justly confer immortality on a man who well deserved so magnificent an eulogium. He was at once a great hero and a great legislator; . . . the variety of his advantages and the different scenes in which he has been engaged make me regret that his life has never been written. His settlement of Georgia gave a greater luster to his character than even his military exploits." Time has not changed this estimate of his character, if we may trust the judgment of Bancroft, who thus describes him:

The gentleness of Oglethorpe's nature appeared in all his actions. He was merciful to the prisoner; a father to the emigrant; the unwavering friend of Wesley; the constant benefactor of the Moravians; honestly zealous for the conversion of the Indians; invoking for the negro the panoply of the Gospel. He was, for a commercial age, the representative of that chivalry which knew neither fear nor reproach, and felt a stain on honor like a wound.

Loyal and brave; choleric yet merciful; versed

James Oglethorpe

in elegant letters; affable even to talkativeness, slightly boastful and tinged with vanity—he was ever ready to shed blood rather than brook an insult, but more ready to expose life for those who looked to him for defense. A monarchist in the state, friendly to the Church, he seemed like one who had survived his times—like the relic of a former century and a more chivalrous age—illustrating to the modern world of business what a crowd of virtues and of charities could cluster around the heart of a cavalier.

Still healthy and vigorous, Oglethorpe could at ninety-five outwalk men not half his age, and to the end his hearing was acute and his eyes undimmed—all of which he attributed as much to his remarkably abstemious life as to his active employments.

He was at last attacked by a violent fever and died at Cranham Hall on the morning of July 1, 1785. His body was laid in the family vault of the Wrights within Cranham Church. Mrs. Oglethorpe placed in the northern wall of the chapel a monumental tablet. The inscription on this tablet, like those found on old tombstones of that day, was lengthy. It sets forth the disposition, affections, virtues, public employments, private charities, even extending to his marriage and giving a hint of his wife's connections and prospects as

Old Age and Death

heiress of a baronet—in fact, a short biography done in marble. Two years later Mrs. Oglethorpe died and was placed beside her adored husband. Her obituary in the Gentlemen's Magazine contained this testimony to her worth:

Very many and continual were her acts of charity and benevolence, but as she would herself been hurt by any display of them in her lifetime, we shall say no more. Not to have mentioned them at all would have been unjust to her memory, and not less so to the world, in which such an example may operate as an incitement to others to go and do likewise.

Few relics of Oglethorpe have been preserved. "His house at St. Simons was destroyed by fire; so also was Cranham Hall, and with it every private record of his life." In the library of Corpus Christi College, Oxford, is a manuscript French version of the Bible, finely illuminated, presented by him to the college; and in Savannah, Ga., was a Bible given by him to the Masonic lodge. He once sat to Reynolds for his portrait by request of the Duke of Rutland, but that picture, with many others of Sir Joshua's, was destroyed by a fire at Belvoir.

There is an engraved likeness of Ogle-

James Oglethorpe

thorpe, taken a few months before his death, when reading without spectacles at the sale of Dr. Johnson's library. One other likeness of the general, with his Indian pupil by his side, was presented by himself to Mr. Noble Jones, of Georgia, but was lost in the capture of Savannah by the British in 1778—a sad loss to the State whose earliest settlers called him "Father." They long hoped for his return, rejoiced in his prosperity, were proud to know that the King had promoted to a generalship their commander-in-chief, and that for many years he was senior general of the British army. The record of his life, so full of benevolence and patriotism pure and unselfish, will ever be a rich legacy to the children of Georgia.

Old Age and Death

INSCRIPTION ON MONUMENTAL TABLET IN CRANHAM CHURCH

Near this place lie the remains of
James Edward Oglethorpe, Esq.,
who served under Prince Eugene, and in
1714 was Captain-Lieutenant in the
1st troop of Queen's Guards.
In 1740 he was appointed Colonel of a regiment
to be raised in Georgia.
In 1745 he was appointed Major-General;
In 1747 Lieutenant-General; and
In 1765 General of His Majesty's forces.
In his civil station he was very early conspicuous.
He was chosen M.P. for Halsmere in Surrey in
1722, and continued to represent it until 1754.
In the Committee of Parliament for enquiring into
the state of the Gaols, formed Feb. 25th, 1728
and of which he was chairman,
the active and preserving zeal of his benevolence
found a truly suitable employment,
by visiting with his colleagues of that generous body,
the dark and pestilential dungeons of the prisons
which at that time dishonored the Metropolis,
detecting the most enormous oppressions;
obtaining exemplary punishment on those
who had been guilty of such outrages against humanity and

James Oglethorpe

  Justice, and restoring multitudes from extreme misery
    to light and freedom.
   Of these, about 700, rendered,
    by long confinement for debt,
strangers and helpless in the country of their birth, and
desirous of seeking an asylum in the wilds of America,
   were by him conducted thither in 1732.
He willingly encountered in their behalf a variety of
    fatigue and danger, and thus became the
    Founder of the Colony of Georgia; which
    (Founded on the ardent wish for liberty)
Set the noble example of prohibiting the importation of slaves.
This new establishment he strenuously and successfully defended
    against a powerful invasion of Spaniards.
In the year in which he quitted England to found this settlement,
   he nobly strove to restore our true national defenses by
     Sea and Land,
A free navy without impressing; a constitutional militia.
   But his sole affections were more enlarged than
     even the term Patriotism can express.
    He was the friend of the oppressed negro;
    No part of the world was too remote,
No interest too unconnected or too opposed to his own,
To prevent his immediate succor of suffering humanity.
    For such qualities he received from the ever
     memorable John, Duke of Argyle,
    a full testimony in the British Senate to
    his military character, his natural generosity,
his contempt of danger, and his regard for the Publick.
A similar encomium is perpetuated in a foreign language;
and, by one of our most celebrated Poets, his remembrance

Old Age and Death

is transmitted to Posterity in lines justly expressive
of the purity, the ardor, the extent of his benevolence.
He lived till the 1st of July 1785,
a venerable instance to what a fulness of duration
and of continued usefulness
a life of temperance and virtuous labor
is capable of being protracted.
His widow, Elizabeth,
Daughter of Sir Nathan Wrighte, Cranham Hall Essex, Bart.,
and only sister and heiress of Sir Samuel Wrighte Bart. of the
same place, surviving with regret
(though with due submission to Divine Providence)
an affectionate husband, after a union of more than 40 years,
hath inscribed to his memory
These faint traces of his excellent character.

AUTHORITIES CONSULTED

BANCROFT: History of the United States.
Biographical Memoirs of Oglethorpe.
CARLYLE: Frederick the Great.
GRANTZ: History of the Moravians.
Gentleman's Magazine, London.
HARRIS: Rise and Progress of the Colony of Georgia.
Hannah More's Letters.
HOLMES: Annals of America.
HILDRETH: History of the United States.
HEWATT: History of Georgia and South Carolina.
JONES: History of Georgia.
LAWSON: Voyage to Carolina.
MOORE: Journal.
MOORE: Life of the Wesleys.
OGLETHORPE: Account of the Provinces South Carolina and Georgia.
ROGERS: Table Talk.
RAY: A Compleat History of the Rebellion.
STEPHENS: Journal of the Proceedings of Georgia.
SPALDING: Collections of Georgia Historical Society.
SALMON: Universal History.
Scott's Magazine, London.
STROBEL: History of the Salzburgers.

Authorities Consulted

THORSBY: History of Leeds.
WRIGHT: Memoir of Oglethorpe.
WESLEY: Journal.
WHITEFIELD: Letters.
VON RECK: Journal.

INDEX

ADAMS, JOHN, 200.
African slave trade, 53; importation of slaves prohibited, 54.
Alligators, 70.
Amelia Island, attacked by Spaniards, 120.
American Revolution, 199.
Annals of America, 200.
Argyle, Duke of, 138.
Authorities consulted, 210.

BANCROFT, GEORGE, description of Oglethorpe, 203.
Bathurst, Sir Thomas, 58.
Belcher, Governor of Massachusetts, congratulations from, 33; ideas of slavery, 55.
Bull, Governor, 162, 163, 176, 178.

CAMPAIGN against the Spanish, 168 et seq.
Carolina Indians, 120.
Carolina traders, 105.
Carolinians, 158, 180.
Castell, Mr., his imprisonment for debt, 9.
Causton, Thomas, deputy-governor of Georgia, 46.
Cherokee Indians, 3, 114, 126, 159.
Chickasaws, allies of Oglethorpe, 110; desert Oglethorpe, 134, 157.
Choctaws, allies of Oglethorpe, 110, 113.

Cochran, Lieutenant - Colonel James, 99.
Colonies attacked by Spanish fleet, 164.
Colonists of Darien and Frederica, 101.
Colony of Carolina, 1.
Colony of Georgia, 15; character of, 17.
Colony of South Carolina, 21.
Compleat Collection of Voyages and Travels, 102.
Cooke, Colonel, 189.
Coquina, 140.
Corpus Christi College, 5.
Council of Safety, 195.
Cranham Church, memorial tablet in, 207.
Cranham Hall, residence of Oglethorpe, 191.
Creek Indians, 71, 87, 124, 157; furnish warriors, 110; treaty with, 112.
Cuming, Sir Alexander, 2; sent as an embassy to the Cherokees, 3.

DARIEN, town of, 58.
Demeré, Captain Raymond, 141.
Dempsey, Mr., commissioner to Spanish Governor of Florida, 71, 72.
Don Francisco del Morale Sanchey, Governor of St. Augustine, 75, 76, 86, 98, 114, 119.

James Oglethorpe

Drake, Sir Francis, 71, 73.
Duke of Cumberland, 192, 193.
Dunbar, Captain George, 183, 186.

EARL OF DARTMOUTH, 54.

Emigration to Georgia, 1732, 13, 14; from Austria, 37, 58.
English Government declares war against Spain, 115; vigorous prosecution of war against Spain, 149, 180.
English Parliament, 53.

FLORIDA Indians, 101.

Fort Argyle, 34, 36.
Fort George, 88.
Fort Moosa, 129.
Fort Picolata, 125.
Fort San Diego, 121, 131, 134.
Fort St. Andrews, residence of Oglethorpe, 105.
Fort St. Francis, 124; surrenders to Oglethorpe, 125.
Fort William, attack upon, repulsed, 174.
Frederica, 36, 78, 84, 140, 142, 175.

GENERAL ASSEMBLY of South Carolina, 114, 123; fails to give succor, 126, 189.

Georgia, history of, by Stevens, 16; deliverance from Spanish, 175.
Georgia colony in great danger, 167.
Georgia orphanage, 143, 144, 145, 147.
Georgia Rangers, 192.
Goldsmith, Oliver, 197.
Gordon, Rev. Alexander, 143.
Governor Bull, refuses assistance to Oglethorpe, 162, 163, 176.
Governor of South Carolina, gives assistance, 27, 183.

Governor of St. Augustine, 75, 76, 86; orders English merchants to leave, 98; instigates revolt among negroes, 114; treaty with, 119.
Guarda-costas of the Spanish, 118.

HABERSHAM, HON. JAMES, 148, 195.

Habersham, Joseph, 194.
Haddock, Admiral, 119.
Hamer Captain, 161, 173.
Hewatt, Dr., Scotch minister, 15.
Highlanders, 58, 89, 121, 168, 196.
Highland Rangers, 124, 131.
History of Georgia, by Stevens, 16.
Horton, Major, 190.
Huss, John, 43.

IMPRISONMENT for debt, 8.

Indian chiefs pledge loyalty to Oglethorpe, 105.
Indians, 66, 67; troubles with, 70; hatred toward the Spaniards, 71; treaty with, 32, 112, 192.
Indians, Lower Creek, 30; treaty with, 32.
Inscription on monumental tablet in Cranham Church, 207.
Israelites, colony of, 35.

JAILS of London, 9, 10, 11.

Jekyll Island, 142.
Jekyll, Joseph, 36.
Johnson, Samuel, 198.
Jones, Colonel Charles, 17.
Jones, Noble, 145, 194.
Journal of the Trustees, 17.

KING OF SPAIN, 95.

LIQUORS, prohibited, 53.

London Daily Post, editorial on Georgia colony, 96.

Index

London jails, horrors of, 9, 10, 11.
Lord Baltimore, 158.
Lower Creek Indians, 30, 100.

MACKAY, ADJUTANT HUGH, 125.
Malachee, "Emperor of the Creeks," 109.
McCall, Hugh, 199.
McPherson, Captain, 34, 123.
Margravate of Azilia, 1.
McIntosh, General Lachlin, 69, 186.
McIntosh, Captain John More 85, 133, 197.
Mellidge, John, 144, 145, 146, 147.
Missionaries to the Indians, 50, 61.
Montgomery, Sir Robert, 1, 2, 12.
Monumental tablet to Oglethorpe, 207.
Moore, Francis, 60.
Moravians, 59, 60, 193.
More Hannah, describes Oglethorpe 202.
Mount Venture, burning of, by Spanish Indians, 179.
Musgrove, Mary, 25.
Mutiny among soldiers, 106.

NEGRO slaves, 53.
Negroes, revolt among, in South Carolina, 114.

OBITUARY of Oglethorpe's wife, 205.
Oglethorpe, James, founder of Georgia, ancestry and early years, 1, 3; succeeds to family estate, 5; birth, 5; education, 5; incident in his young soldier life, 5; enters English army as ensign, 6; goes to the Continent and enlists, 6; elected to Parliament, 8; chairman of committee on prisons, 9; petitions throne for charter, 12; publishes essays, 12; leaves England with colony, 20; authorized to act as Colonial Governor, 21; arrival at Charleston, 21; explores Savannah River, 22; makes stringent laws against sale of intoxicating liquors, 22; letter to trustees, 23; interview with Tomo Chichi, 25; describes Georgia province, 25; makes address to General Assembly of South Carolina, 29; excursion to interior, 33; explores southern coast, 35; offers home to Salzburgers, 38; returns to England, 1734, 47; enthusiastically welcomed, 47; The Christian Hero, 47; estimate of Indian character, 48; advocates laws for Georgia, 53; his ideas of slavery, 55; returns to Georgia, 61; issues proclamation to maintain peace with Indians, 66; builds fort at St. Simons, 68; returns to Tybee, 69; instructs colonists in planting, 70; troubles with the Indians, 73; returns to Frederica, 76; suspects Spaniards of treachery, 76; increasing cares, 79; strengthens his defenses, 80; prepares for an attack by Spaniards, 81; goes to St. Andrews, 82; prevents attack by Spanish by a ruse, 85; letter to Lieutenant-Governor of South Carolina and to Governor of New York, 88; interview with Spanish commissioners, 91; letter to trustees, 91; goes to Savannah, 93; concludes a treaty with Governor of St. Augustine, 94; sails for England, November, 1736, 95; cordial reception, 95; asks for military force, 96; appointed general, 98; returns to Georgia, 99; further plans for defense,

100; discovers treachery in camp, 102; makes residence at Fort St. Andrews, 105; attacked by mutinous soldiers, 106; goes to Charleston, 107; foresees war between England and Spain and with France, 107; journey to the interior, 109; description of journey, 109; concludes treaty with Indians, 112; gratifying success of his mission, 113; prostrated with fever at Fort Augusta, 114; protects South Carolina colonists from negroes, 115; announces declaration of war by England against Spain, 115; musters his military force, 117; inspects southern frontier, 118; fortifies Frederica, 121; lacks war supplies, 121; invades Florida, 121; asks for more troops, 122; plans to assault St. Augustine, 128; abandons the siege, 135; criticised by Charleston newspapers, 136; praised by citizens, 137; letter to Under-Secretary, 139; his home at Frederica, 141; letter to Duke of Newcastle, May, 1741, 150; delay in getting supplies, 153; appeals to Home Government, 154; attacks Spanish privateers, 155; influence over native tribes, 157; his great abilities, 158; letter to Duke of Newcastle, June, 1742, 160; escapes from Spanish fleet, 165; his successful stratagem, 172; great victory over Spanish fleet, 175; praised by people of Port Royal, 176; doubts that the war is over, 177; again appeals to Home Government, 179; attacks Spaniards at St. Johns, 181; meets with a nearly fatal accident, 182; returns to England, July, 1743, 186; venomously attacked by Vanderdussen, 189; appointed general officer, 191; his marriage, 191; promoted to rank of major-general, 192; joins Duke of Cumberland's forces, 192; made lieutenant-general, 193; remonstrates against cruelties on prisoners, 193; court-martialed and acquitted, 193; his high sense of justice, 194; end of public career, 1754, 197; letter to Oliver Goldsmith, 197; refuses command of forces to subdue colonists, 199; expresses regard for America, 200; his death, 1785, 204; likeness of, 205.

Oglethorpe, Mrs., wife of James Oglethorpe, death of, 205.

Onechachumpa, Indian warrior, 31.

PALMER, COLONEL, commanding Highlanders, 132; killed at Fort Moosa, 133.
Parliament, English, 8, 188.
Pease, Commodore, 134, 135.
Penn, William, 15, 158.
Pretender, the, 6, 187, 193.
Prison reform, 8.

RAMSEY'S History of South Carolina, 135, 137.
Richards, Major, 75, 80, 85.
Royal African Company, 54.
Rutledge, Andrew, Chief Justice of South Carolina, 182.

ST. ANDREWS, Fort, 72.
St. Augustine, consternation at Fort, 87, 125; attacked by Oglethorpe, 128.
St. Johns River, 72.
St. Matthias River, 124.
St. Simons, 35, 58, 66, 70, 142, 166; batteries destroyed, 167, 173.

Index

Salzburg, 37.
Salzburgers, 38, 39, 41; described by Carlyle, 42, 43, 44, 58, 196.
San Diego, attack upon, 127; surrender of, 128.
Savannah, described by Oglethorpe, 23; population in 1733, 34; rapid improvement of, 62; arrival of troops in, 98.
Scotch Highlanders, 64, 65, 68; build fort at Darien, 69.
Seal of colony of Georgia, 17.
Selina, Countess Dowager of Huntingdon, 149.
Settlers, laws regarding, 57, 63.
Silk industry, 18, 56, 59, 62, 63, 103.
Similli, Creek chief, 184.
Sir Francis Drake, 71, 73.
Six Nations, 157.
Slavery discouraged, 19, 55.
Sotolycate, Indian deity, 30.
South Carolina General Assembly, 107, 114.
South Carolina Gazette, impressions of Oglethorpe, 26.
South Sea Bubble, 2.
Spain, court of, demands recall of Oglethorpe, 96.
Spalding, Thomas, 141.
Spaniards of Florida, 34.
Spaniards, threatened invasion by, 80; attempt to bribe the Indians, 109; barbarous conduct of, 120; surrender to Oglethorpe, 125; endeavor to excite revolt among negroes, 161.
Spanish privateers, 155, 159.
Stone, Under-Secretary Andrew, 139.
Sutton, Lady Eleanor, mother of Oglethorpe, 4.
Sutton of Oglethorpe, grandfather to Oglethorpe, 4.
Sutton, Sir Theophilus, father of Oglethorpe, 4.

TOMO CHICHI, chief of the Yamacraws and faithful friend of Oglethorpe, 24, 31, 32; goes to England, 46, 56, 65, 66, 71, 73; his illness, 104, 110; death and funeral honors, 117.
Tooanahowi, successor of Tomo Chichi, 127, 168.
Traitors, punished, 102.
Treaty with Indians, 32.
Troubles in Florida, 118.
Tschatschi, King, 59.
Tybee Island, 61.

UCHEES, 66.
United Brethren, 59; history of, 59, 193.

VANDERDUSSEN, CAPTAIN ALEXANDER, 131, 136, 164, 189.
Vernon, Admiral, 150, 188.

WALPOLE, HORACE, impressions of Oglethorpe, 200, 201.
War with Spain, 153.
War-dance, 105.
Washington, George, 141, 202.
Wesley, Charles, missionary to Georgia, his overofficiousness, 68, 93; resigns as secretary and returns to England, 94, 95.
Wesley, John, missionary to Georgia, 51.
Wesley, Rev. Samuel, 50.
Wesley's journal, 82, 83.
Westbrook mansion, 6; traditions of, 7.
Whitefield, Rev. George, 98, 142, 143, 147; letter to Oglethorpe 148; death of, 149, 175.

YAMACRAW BLUFF, 22.
"Young Pretender," 192.

HISTORIC LIVES SERIES.

A series of popular biographies dealing with famous men of all times and countries, written in brief form and representing the latest knowledge on the subjects, each illustrated with appropriate full-page pictures, the authors being chosen for their special knowledge of the subjects.

Each 12mo, Illustrated, Cloth, $1.00 net.
Postage, 10 cents additional.

NOW READY.

Father Marquette, the Explorer of the Mississippi.
By REUBEN GOLD THWAITES, Editor of "The Jesuit Relations," etc.

Daniel Boone.
By REUBEN GOLD THWAITES, Editor of "The Jesuit Relations," "Father Marquette," etc.

Horace Greeley.
By WILLIAM A. LINN, Author of "The Story of the Mormons."

Sir William Johnson.
By AUGUSTUS C. BUELL, Author of "Paul Jones, Founder of the American Navy."

Anthony Wayne.
By JOHN R. SPEARS.

Champlain: The Founder of New France.
By EDWIN ASA DIX, M.A., LL.D., Formerly Fellow in History in Princeton University; Author of "Deacon Bradbury," "A Midsummer Drive through the Pyrenees," etc.

OTHERS IN PREPARATION.

D. APPLETON AND COMPANY, NEW YORK.

BOOKS BY DR. EDWARD EGGLESTON.

The Beginners of a Nation.

A History of the Source and Rise of the Earliest English Settlements in America, with Special Reference to the Life and Character of the People. The first volume in A History of Life in the United States. Small 8vo. Gilt top, uncut, with Maps. Cloth, $1.50.

"The delightful style, the clear flow of the narrative, the philosophical tone, and the able analysis of men and events will commend Mr. Eggleston's work to earnest students."—*Philadelphia Public Ledger.*

"The work is worthy of careful reading, not only because of the author's ability as a literary artist, but because of his conspicuous proficiency in interpreting the causes of and changes in American life and character."—*Boston Journal.*

"Few works on the period which it covers can compare with this in point of mere literary attractiveness, and we fancy that many to whom its scholarly value will not appeal will read the volume with interest and delight."—*New York Evening Post.*

"Written with a firm grasp of the theme, inspired by ample knowledge, and made attractive by a vigorous and resonant style, the book will receive much attention. It is a great theme the author has taken up, and he grasps it with the confidence of a master."—*New York Times.*

The Transit of Civilization,

From England to America in the Seventeenth Century. Uniform with "The Beginners of a Nation." Small 8vo. Gilt top, uncut. Cloth, $1.50.

"Every subject is treated with tolerance and yet with a comprehensive grasp."—*Boston Globe.*

"It places the whole history of colonial life in an entirely new and fascinating light."—*New York Commercial Advertiser.*

"No such account has ever been given of the colonists, and no such view exists of England in the seventeenth century."—*Brooklyn Eagle.*

"This is beyond question one of the most important examples of culture history ever published in this country. Many of the themes which are treated have never been presented before in anything like an adequate manner."—*Philadelphia Press.*

D. APPLETON AND COMPANY, NEW YORK.

EXPANSION OF THE REPUBLIC SERIES.

In this series the purpose is to show what have been the great developing forces in the making of the United States as we now know them. Not only will territorial subjects be dealt with, but political, racial, and industrial. It is an important series, and the reception already accorded to it gives promise of real distinction for the entire set.

Each volume 12mo, Illustrated, $1.25 net.
Postage, 12 cents additional.

NOW READY.

The History of the Louisiana Purchase.
By JAMES K. HOSMER, Ph.D., LL.D.

Ohio and her Western Reserve.
By ALFRED MATHEWS.

The History of Puerto Rico.
By R. A. VAN MIDDELDYK. With an Introduction, etc., by Prof. Martin G. Brumbaugh.

Steps in the Expansion of our Territory.
By OSCAR PHELPS AUSTIN, Chief of the Bureau of Statistics, Treasury Department.

Rocky Mountain Exploration.
By REUBEN GOLD THWAITES, Superintendent of the State Historical Society of Wisconsin.

IN PREPARATION.

The Conquest of the Southwest.
By CYRUS TOWNSEND BRADY, Author of "Paul Jones," in the Great Commanders Series.

The Purchase of Alaska.
By OSCAR PHELPS AUSTIN, Chief of the Bureau of Statistics, Treasury Department.

PROPOSED VOLUMES.

The Settlement of the Pacific Coast.
The Founding of Chicago and the Development of the Middle West.
John Brown and the Troubles in Kansas.

D. APPLETON AND COMPANY, NEW YORK.

GREAT COMMANDERS.

Edited by General JAMES GRANT WILSON.

This series forms one of the most notable collections of books that has been published for many years. The success it has met with since the first volume was issued, and the widespread attention it has attracted, indicate that it has satisfactorily fulfilled its purpose, viz., to provide in a popular form and moderate compass the records of the lives of men who have been conspicuously eminent in the great conflicts that established American independence and maintained our national integrity and unity. Each biography has been written by an author especially well qualified for the task, and the result is not only a series of fascinating stories of the lives and deeds of great men, but a rich mine of valuable information for the student of American history and biography.

Each, 12mo, cloth, gilt top, $1.50 net.
Postage, 11 cents additional.

NOW READY.

Admiral Farragut - - - - By Captain A. T. MAHAN, U. S. N.
General Taylor - - - - - By General O. O. HOWARD, U. S. A.
General Jackson - - - - - - - - - - By JAMES PARTON.
General Greene - - - - - - By General FRANCIS V. GREENE.
General J. E. Johnston - - By ROBERT M. HUGHES, of Virginia.
General Thomas - - - - - - - By HENRY COPPEE, LL. D.
General Scott - - - - - - - By General MARCUS J. WRIGHT.
General Washington - - - By General BRADLEY T. JOHNSON.
General Lee - - - - - - - - - By General FITZHUGH LEE.
General Hancock - - - - - By General FRANCIS A. WALKER.
General Sheridan - - - - - By General HENRY E. DAVIES.
General Grant - - - - - By General JAMES GRANT WILSON.
General Sherman - - - - - By General MANNING F. FORCE.
Commodore Paul Jones - - - - By CYRUS TOWNSEND BRADY.
General Meade - - - - - - - - By ISAAC R. PENNYPACKER.
General McClellan - - - - - By General PETER S. MICHIE.
General Forrest - - - - - - By Captain J. HARVEY MATHES.
Admiral Porter - By JAMES R. SOLEY, late Assistant Secretary U. S. Navy.

D. APPLETON AND COMPANY, NEW YORK.

By EDGAR STANTON MACLAY, A. M.

A History of the United States Navy. (1775 to 1902.)—New and revised edition.

In three volumes, the new volume containing an Account of the Navy since the Civil War, with a history of the Spanish-American War revised to the date of this edition, and an Account of naval operations in the Philippines, etc. Technical Revision of the first two volumes by Lieutenant ROY C. SMITH, U. S. N. Illustrated. 8vo. Cloth, $3.00 net per volume ; postage, 26 cents per volume additional.

In the new edition of Vol. III, which is now ready for publication, the author brings his History of the Navy down to the present time. In the prefaces of the volumes of this history the author has expressed and emphasized his desire for suggestions, new information, and corrections which might be utilized in perfecting his work. He has, therefore, carefully studied the evidence brought out at the recent Schley Court of Inquiry, and while the findings of that Court were for the most part in accordance with the results of his own historical investigations, he has modified certain portions of his narrative. Whatever opinions may be held regarding any phases of our recent naval history, the fact remains that the industry, care, and thoroughness, which were unanimously praised by newspaper reviewers and experts in the case of the first two volumes, have been sedulously applied to the preparation of this new edition of the third volume.

A History of American Privateers.

Uniform with "A History of the United States Navy." One volume. Illustrated. 8vo. Cloth, $3.00 net ; postage, 24 cents additional.

After several years of research the distinguished historian of American sea power presents the first comprehensive account of one of the most picturesque and absorbing phases of our maritime warfare. The importance of the theme is indicated by the fact that the value of prizes and cargoes taken by privateers in the Revolution was three times that of the prizes and cargoes taken by naval vessels, while in the War of 1812 we had 517 privateers and only 23 vessels in our navy. Mr. Maclay's romantic tale is accompanied by reproductions of contemporary pictures, portraits, and documents, and also by illustrations by Mr. George Gibbs.

The Private Journal of William Maclay,

United States Senator from Pennsylvania, 1789-1791. With Portrait from Original Miniature. Edited by EDGAR STANTON MACLAY, A. M. Large 8vo. Cloth, $2.25.

During his two years in the Senate William Maclay kept a journal of his own in which he minutely recorded the transactions of each day. This record throws a flood of light on the doings of our first legislators.

D. APPLETON AND COMPANY, NEW YORK.

THE STORY OF THE WEST SERIES.
Edited by RIPLEY HITCHCOCK.

The Story of the Trapper.

By A. C. LAUT, Author of "Heralds of Empire." Illustrated by Heming. 12mo. Cloth, $1.25 net; postage, 12 cents additional.

> "A delightfully spirited book."—*Brooklyn Eagle.*
> "A rarely instructive and entertaining book."—*New York World.*
> "Unexpectedly good."—*Boston Herald.*
> "Instructive and carefully prepared."—*Chicago News.*
> "Excellent reading wherever one dips into it."—*Cleveland Leader.*

OTHER VOLUMES.
Illustrated. 12mo. Cloth, each, $1.50.

The Story of the Soldier.

By General G. A. FORSYTH, U. S. Army (retired). Illustrated by R. F. Zogbaum.

The Story of the Railroad.

By CY WARMAN, Author of "The Express Messenger," etc. With Maps and many Illustrations by B. West Clinedinst and from photographs.

The Story of the Cowboy.

By E. HOUGH, Author of "The Singing Mouse Stories," etc. Illustrated by William L. Wells and C. M. Russell.

> "Mr. Hough is to be thanked for having written so excellent a book. The cowboy story, as this author has told it, will be the cowboy's fitting eulogy. This volume will be consulted in years to come as an authority on past conditions of the far West. For fine literary work the author is to be highly complimented. Here, certainly, we have a choice piece of writing."—*New York Times.*

The Story of the Mine.

As illustrated by the Great Comstock Lode of Nevada. By CHARLES HOWARD SHINN.

> "The author has written a book not alone full of information, but replete with the true romance of the American mine."—*New York Times.*

The Story of the Indian.

By GEORGE BIRD GRINNELL, Author of "Pawnee Hero Stories," "Blackfoot Lodge Tales," etc.

> "Only an author qualified by personal experience could offer us a profitable study of a race so alien from our own as is the Indian in thought, feeling, and culture. Only long association with Indians can enable a white man measurably to comprehend their thoughts and enter into their feelings. Such association has been Mr. Grinnell's."—*New York Sun.*

D. APPLETON AND COMPANY, NEW YORK.

THE AUTHENTIC LIFE OF LINCOLN.

Abraham Lincoln: The True Story of a Great Life.

By WILLIAM H. HERNDON and JESSE W. WEIK. With numerous Illustrations. New and revised edition, with an Introduction by Horace White. In two volumes. 12mo. Cloth, $3.00.

This is probably the most intimate life of Lincoln ever written. The book, by Lincoln's law-partner, William H. Herndon, and his friend Jesse W. Weik, shows us Lincoln the man. It is a true picture of his surroundings and influences and acts. It is not an attempt to construct a political history, with Lincoln often in the background, nor is it an effort to apotheosize the American who stands first in our history next to Washington. The writers knew Lincoln intimately. Their book is the result of unreserved association; hence, it has taken rank as the best and most illuminating study of Lincoln's character and personality.

"Truly, they who wish to know Lincoln as he really was must read the biography by his friend and law-partner, W. H. Herndon. This book was imperatively needed to brush aside the rank growth of myth and legend which was threatening to hide the real lineaments of Lincoln from the eyes of posterity. . . . There is no doubt about the faithfulness of Mr. Herndon's delineation. The marks of unflinching veracity are patent in every line."—*New York Sun.*

"The three portraits of Lincoln are the best that exist; and not the least characteristic of these, the Lincoln of the Douglas debates, has never before been engraved. . . . Herndon's narrative gives, as nothing else is likely to give, the material from which we may form a true picture of the man from infancy to maturity."—*The Nation.*

"Mr. Herndon is naturally a very direct writer, and he has been industrious in gathering material. Whether an incident happened before or behind the scenes, is all the same to him. He gives it without artifice or apology. He describes the life of his friend Lincoln just as he saw it."—*Cincinnati Commercial Gazette.*

"A remarkable piece of literary achievement—remarkable alike for its fidelity to facts, its fulness of details, its constructive skill, and its literary charm."—*New York Times.*

"It will always remain the authentic life of Abraham Lincoln."—*Chicago Herald.*

Lincoln in Story.

The Life of the Martyr President told in Authenticated Anecdotes. Edited by SILAS G. PRATT. Illustrated. 12mo. Cloth, 75 cents net; postage, 9 cents additional.

"An excellent compilation on a subject of which the American people never grow tired."—*Boston Transcript.*

"A valuable and exceedingly interesting addition to Lincoln literature."—*Brooklyn Standard-Union.*

D. APPLETON AND COMPANY, NEW YORK.

"EVERY AMERICAN SHOULD READ IT."
—*The News, Providence.*

The Life and Times of Thomas Jefferson.

By THOMAS E. WATSON, Author of "The Story of France," "Napoleon," etc. Illustrated with many Portraits and Views. 8vo. Attractively bound, $2.50 net; postage, 17 cents additional.

Mr. Watson long since acquired a national reputation in connection with his political activities in Georgia. He startled the public soon afterward by the publication of a history of France, which at once attracted attention quite as marked, though different in kind. His book became interesting not alone as the production of a Southern man interested in politics, but as an entirely original conception of a great theme. There was no question that a life of Jefferson from the hands of such a writer would command very general attention, and the publishers had no sooner announced the work as in preparation than negotiations were begun with the author by two of the best-known newspapers in America for its publication in serial form. During the past summer the appearance of the story in this way has created widespread comment which has now been drawn to the book just published.

Opinions by some of the Leading Papers.

"A vastly entertaining polemic. It directs attention to many undoubtedly neglected facts which writers of the North have ignored or minimized."
—*The New York Times Saturday Review of Books.*

"A noble work. It may well stand on the shelf beside Morley's 'Gladstone' and other epochal biographical works that have come into prominence. It is deeply interesting and thoroughly fair and just."
—*The Globe-Democrat, St. Louis.*

"The book shows great research and is as complete as it could possibly be, and every American should read it."—*The News, Providence.*

"A unique historical work."—*The Commercial Advertiser, New York.*

"Valuable as an historical document and as a witness to certain great facts in the past life of the South which have seldom been acknowledged by historians."—*The Post, Louisville.*

D. APPLETON AND COMPANY, NEW YORK.

"THE MOST UNFORTUNATE WOMAN IN MODERN HISTORY."

Lucretia Borgia: According to Original Documents and Correspondence of Her Day.

By FERDINAND GREGOROVIUS, Author of "A History of the City of Rome in the Middle Ages." Translated from the Third German Edition by John Leslie Garner. Illustrated. 8vo. Cloth, $2.25 net; postage, 17 cents additional.

Lucretia Borgia is the most unfortunate woman in modern history. Is this because she was guilty of the most hideous crimes, or is it simply because she has been unjustly condemned by the world to bear its curse? The question has never been answered. Mankind is ever ready to discover the personification of human virtues and human vices in certain typical characters found in history and fable. The Borgias will never cease to fascinate the historian and the psychologist. They are a satire on a great form or phase of religion, debasing and destroying it. They stand on high pedestals, and from their presence radiates the light of the Christian ideal. In this form we behold and recognize them. We view their acts through a medium which is permeated with religious ideas. Without this, and placed on a purely secular stage, the Borgias would have fallen into a position much less conspicuous than that of many other men, and would soon have ceased to be anything more than representatives of a large species. This is the first translation from the German of this important work of Gregorovius, in which a vast supply of information is furnished about the family of this famous and interesting woman and about herself. The book is illustrated with portraits and views, and offers valuable knowledge upon the times and character of a woman about whose nature a conflict of opinions has raged for centuries. About her beauty and talents there are no two voices; on the question of her vices the world has become divided. A patron of art and letters, as to her private life the most hideous stories gained circulation, making her name the most notorious of her renowned house, not excepting that of her brother, the infamous Cesare Borgia.

In this translation English readers are offered the best known account of this celebrated woman, written by the author of that monumental and illuminating work, "The History of Rome in the Middle Ages."

"The story is far more exciting than most romances, and treats of Italian history and life about which comparatively little that is authoritative can be found in English."—*The Sun, New York.*

D. APPLETON AND COMPANY, NEW YORK.

A TIMELY BOOK.

China.

Travels and Investigations in the "Middle Kingdom"—A Study of its Civilization and Possibilities. Together with an Account of the Boxer War, the Relief of the Legations, and the Re-establishment of Peace. By JAMES HARRISON WILSON, A. M., LL. D., late Major-General United States Volunteers, and Brevet Major-General United States Army. Third edition, revised throughout, enlarged, and reset. 12mo. Cloth, $1.75.

General Wilson's second visit to China and his recent active service in that country have afforded exceptional chances for a knowledge of present conditions and the possibilities of the future. In the light of the information thus obtained at first hand in the country itself, General Wilson is enabled to write with a peculiar authoritativeness in this edition, which brings his study of China down to the present day. In addition to the new chapters which have been added explaining the origin and development of the Boxer insurrection, the relief of the legations, and the outlook for the future, the author has revised his book throughout, and has added much valuable matter in the course of his narrative. This book, which is therefore in many respects new, puts the reader in possession of a broad and comprehensive knowledge of Chinese affairs, and this includes the latest phases of the subject. The practical and discriminating character of the author's study of China will be appreciated more than ever at this time when practical questions relating to Chinese administration, commerce, and other matters of the first importance, are engaging so much attention. This new edition is indispensable for any one who wishes a compact, authoritative presentation of the China of to-day.

D. APPLETON AND COMPANY, NEW YORK.

Trieste

Trieste Publishing has a massive catalogue of classic book titles. Our aim is to provide readers with the highest quality reproductions of fiction and non-fiction literature that has stood the test of time. The many thousands of books in our collection have been sourced from libraries and private collections around the world.

The titles that Trieste Publishing has chosen to be part of the collection have been scanned to simulate the original. Our readers see the books the same way that their first readers did decades or a hundred or more years ago. Books from that period are often spoiled by imperfections that did not exist in the original. Imperfections could be in the form of blurred text, photographs, or missing pages. It is highly unlikely that this would occur with one of our books. Our extensive quality control ensures that the readers of Trieste Publishing's books will be delighted with their purchase. Our staff has thoroughly reviewed every page of all the books in the collection, repairing, or if necessary, rejecting titles that are not of the highest quality. This process ensures that the reader of one of Trieste Publishing's titles receives a volume that faithfully reproduces the original, and to the maximum degree possible, gives them the experience of owning the original work.

We pride ourselves on not only creating a pathway to an extensive reservoir of books of the finest quality, but also providing value to every one of our readers. Generally, Trieste books are purchased singly - on demand, however they may also be purchased in bulk. Readers interested in bulk purchases are invited to contact us directly to enquire about our tailored bulk rates. Email: customerservice@triestepublishing.com

You May Also Like

A ride to Niagara in 1809

Thomas Cooper

ISBN: 9781760576271
Paperback: 56 pages
Dimensions: 6.14 x 0.12 x 9.21 inches
Language: eng

Honoré de Balzac

Albert Keim & Louis Lumet & Frederic Taber Cooper

ISBN: 9780649312313
Paperback: 292 pages
Dimensions: 6.14 x 0.61 x 9.21 inches
Language: eng

www.triestepublishing.com

You May Also Like

The spy; a tale of the neutral ground. In two volumes. Vol. I

James Fenimore Cooper

ISBN: 9780649294695
Paperback: 278 pages
Dimensions: 6.14 x 0.58 x 9.21 inches
Language: eng

Ned Myers, or, A life before the mast

J. Fenimore Cooper

ISBN: 9780649016181
Paperback: 250 pages
Dimensions: 6.14 x 0.53 x 9.21 inches
Language: eng

www.triestepublishing.com

You May Also Like

Shut Your Mouth and Save Your Life

George Catlin

ISBN: 9781760570491
Paperback: 118 pages
Dimensions: 6.14 x 0.25 x 9.21 inches
Language: eng

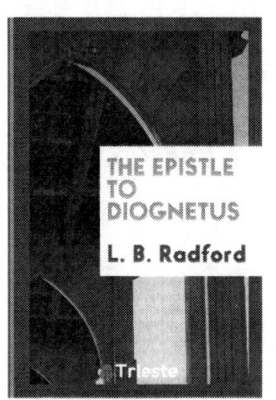

The Epistle to Diognetus

L. B. Radford

ISBN: 9781760570934
Paperback: 106 pages
Dimensions: 6.14 x 0.22 x 9.21 inches
Language: eng

www.triestepublishing.com

You May Also Like

Bulgarian horrors and the question of the East

W. E. Gladstone

ISBN: 9781760571146
Paperback: 46 pages
Dimensions: 6.14 x 0.09 x 9.21 inches
Language: eng

Snow-bound: A Winter Idyl

John Greenleaf Whittier

ISBN: 9781760571528
Paperback: 64 pages
Dimensions: 5.5 x 0.13 x 8.25 inches
Language: eng

Find more of our titles on our website. We have a selection of thousands of titles that will interest you. Please visit

www.triestepublishing.com